$4 \times 7 - 3 > 0 \div 8 + 2 \times 6 < 1 \div 5 + 9 - 4 \times 7 - 3 > 0 \div 8 + 2 \times 6 < 1 \div 5 + 9$

40 Easy-to-Make Math Manipulatives

by Carole J. Reesink

SCHOLASTIC
PROFESSIONAL BOOKS

New York • Toronto • London • Auckland • Sydney
Mexico City • New Delhi • Hong Kong • Buenos Aires

Cover design by Josué Castilleja

Interior design by Sydney Wright

Interior illustrations by Kate Flanagan

ISBN 0-439-36532-5

Copyright © 2003 by Carole J. Reesink

Published by Scholastic Inc.

Printed in the U.S.A.

1 2 3 4 5 6 7 8 9 10   40   09 08 07 06 05 04 03

Contents

Measurement

Time & Money

Geometry, Patterns & Fractions

Data Analysis, Probability & Reasoning

Introduction

Welcome to *40 Easy-to-Make Math Manipulatives*! In this book, you will find inexpensive, easy-to-make math projects that can be used with your students to introduce, teach, and reinforce essential math skills.

The sturdy, long-lasting projects in *40 Easy-to-Make Math Manipulatives* use materials that are readily available, or can be obtained at little or no expense. From the Wonderful 100s Board and Perky Pig Computer to Magnetic Coin Keepers and Geometric Holiday Ornaments, you'll find projects that fit—and help stretch—your classroom budget while providing fun, interactive ways for students to learn and practice the skills they need to know.

Derived from a series of successful workshops, these innovative, teacher-tested projects are based on math skills that correlate with the standards recommended by the National Council of Teachers of Mathematics. (See Connections With the NCTM Standards on pages 6–7.) Whether you're teaching basic number skills, fractions, or graphing, there's a project in this book to address the targeted concept!

Each project itemizes related math concepts and includes a complete list of materials, detailed directions on making the project, management tips, ways to use the project with students, and, where applicable, reproducible patterns. In some cases, additional ideas and variations for making and using the project are provided.

Pick a project and get started. You'll enjoy making these math manipulatives almost as much as watching your students engage in the fun, meaningful learning that results from your efforts!

Tips for Getting Started

- ◼ In advance, gather all materials needed to make the project.

- ◼ Prepare your work space. If you plan to construct or paint a project outdoors, first check for suitable weather conditions.

- ◼ Many of the projects use common craft items, recyclable containers, or inexpensive materials that can be found at home-improvement, craft, or school-supply stores. Some retailers may be willing to reduce the cost of materials or even donate them for classroom use.

- ◼ Feel free to modify or customize projects to meet your students' specific needs.

- ◼ Most of the projects can be used as math center activities to reinforce math concepts with students. Be sure students have been introduced to the project and understand how to use it before placing it in the math center.

Connections With the NCTM Standards 2000

	Number and Operations	Estimation*	Number Sense and Numeration*	Concepts of Whole-Number Operations*	Whole-Number Computations*	Patterns, Functions, and Algebra*	Fractions and Decimals*	Geometry and Spatial Sense	Data Analysis, Statistics, and Probability	Measurement	Problem Solving	Reasoning and Proof	Communication	Connections	Representation
Wonderful 100s Board		•	•	•	•							•	•	•	•
Clip-On Petal Counters		•	•	•	•							•	•	•	•
Glitter Concept Gloves		•	•	•	•							•	•	•	•
Hex-Nut Counting Stairs		•	•	•	•							•	•	•	•
Mathville Paper Bag Community		•	•									•	•	•	•
Ten-Count Pegboard		•	•	•	•							•	•	•	•
Count 'n' Cliposaurus		•	•	•	•							•	•	•	•
Dinosaur Eggs		•	•	•	•							•	•	•	•
T-rex Number Track		•	•	•	•	•						•	•	•	•
Daisy Counting Garden		•	•	•	•							•	•	•	•
Cool Cup 'n' Straw Counters		•	•	•	•							•	•	•	•
Stepping Stones		•	•	•	•							•	•	•	•
Perfect 100s Pegboard		•	•	•	•					•		•	•	•	•
Zip & Skip Number Line		•		•	•				•		•	•	•	•	•
Number Comparison Dino Puppet		•	•	•	•							•	•	•	•
Mini Math Boards		•		•	•			•			•	•	•	•	•
Computation Cookies		•		•	•		•				•	•	•	•	•
Perky Pig Computer		•		•	•						•	•	•	•	•
Monster Math-Muncher Machine		•		•	•	•	•				•	•	•	•	•
Pizza Multiplication Wheels		•		•	•							•	•	•	•

* Indicates a subcategory of Number and Operations

	Number and Operations	Estimation*	Number Sense and Numeration*	Concepts of Whole-Number Operations*	Whole-Number Computations*	Fractions and Decimals*	Patterns, Functions, and Algebra	Geometry and Spatial Sense	Measurement	Data Analysis, Statistics, and Probability	Problem Solving	Reasoning and Proof	Communication	Connections	Representation
Nifty Nonstandard Rulers	•	•	•						•		•	•	•	•	•
Checkered Measurement Boards	•	•	•	•	•			•	•		•	•	•	•	•
Chocolate Square Geometry	•	•		•	•			•	•		•	•	•	•	•
Sugar-Cube Volume Boxes	•	•						•	•		•	•	•		•
Milk-Jug Measurement Family	•	•	•	•	•	•			•		•	•	•	•	•
Liquid Liter Lizard	•	•	•	•					•		•	•	•	•	•
Giant Magnetic Clock									•		•	•	•	•	•
Magnificent Magnetic Clocks						•					•	•	•	•	•
Digital Zipper Clock											•	•	•	•	•
Giant Magnetic Money	•		•	•	•						•	•	•	•	•
Magnetic Coin Keepers	•		•	•	•	•					•	•	•	•	•
Jiffy Geometric Wallpaper Squares								•		•	•	•	•	•	•
Terrific Tiles								•		•	•	•	•	•	•
Necktie Pattern Busy Board								•		•	•	•	•	•	•
Geometric Holiday Ornaments	•		•	•	•			•	•		•	•	•	•	•
Individual Geoboards	•		•	•				•			•	•	•	•	•
Giant Fraction Magnets	•		•			•					•	•	•	•	•
Linoleum Dominoes	•		•	•	•			•	•		•	•	•	•	•
Probability Clothes Dryer										•	•	•	•	•	•
Velcro Bar Graph	•		•	•						•	•	•	•	•	•

* Indicates a subcategory of Number and Operations

Wonderful 100s Board

This easy-to-make numbers board is a durable, low-cost alternative to commercial 100s boards.

Skills and Concepts

- counting
- one-to-one correspondence
- place value
- addition
- subtraction

Materials

- 9 copies of the large number board pattern, page 10
- 7 copies of the small number board pattern, page 10
- 1 2-foot square of $\frac{3}{4}$-inch thick plywood
- fine-grade sandpaper
- pencil
- ruler
- scissors
- tape
- hammer
- 100 one-pound finishing nails, 2 inches in length
- spray paint
- 2 sets of 1-inch self-adhesive vinyl numerals (1–10)
- 100 1-inch key tags
- black fine-point permanent marker

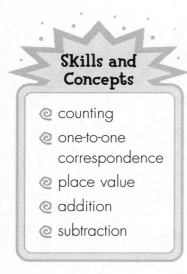

Making the Wonderful 100s Board

1 Sand the plywood to smooth the surface and edges.

2 Use a pencil and ruler to draw a line two inches from each edge of the board.

3 Cut out the number board patterns. Starting at the upper left corner, tape the nine large cutouts end-to-end on the board to cover the inside of the penciled square. Tape three smaller cutouts along the bottom line, and another three along the line on the right of the board. Cut along the dotted line on the last pattern. Tape the single dot in the bottom right corner of the square. When finished, a 100-dot grid will fill the inside of the penciled square.

4 Hammer a nail into the board at each dot, driving the nail through the paper and deep into the wood. Once the nails have been hammered into the board, remove the paper patterns.

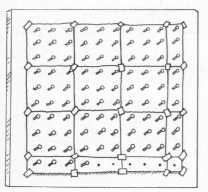

5 Paint the board outdoors or in a well-ventilated area. Allow the paint to dry thoroughly.

6 Attach one set of numerals, in sequence, to the top of each column of nails. Then affix the other set, in sequence, next to the first nail in each row.

7 Use the permanent marker to label each key tag with a numeral from 1 to 100.

HANDY HINTS

▲ If you prefer, paint the board a light color, then use a permanent marker to label the numerals for each column and row directly on the board.

▲ Flat plastic milk-jug lids can be substituted for the key tags. Simply bore a hole in each lid, then label with a numeral.

Ways to Use the Wonderful 100s Board

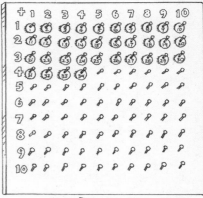

◆ Have children place the key tags one at a time on the board, counting each one as it is hung on the nail. For a variation, hang each key tag on its corresponding nail, leaving an occasional nail empty. Have children count up to each missing numeral and hang the appropriate key tag on the nail.

◆ For practice in place value, hang key tags on the board up to a specified number. Ask children to use the columns and rows to help them report the number in tens and ones. Or prepare note-cards with numerals written as sets of tens and ones. Have children fill in key tags on the board to represent the numerals on the cards.

◆ To provide addition practice, place a quantity of key tags (23, for example) on the board. Then have children add a set of key tags (six, for example) to the board. After they count and place the key tags on the board, ask children to report the sum of the two quantities (29, in this example). To extend, have children write an equation for each addition problem they solve.

◆ Conversely, children can practice subtraction skills by removing key tags from the board. After hanging a set of key tags on the board, have children remove a given quantity and report the remaining number. Ask them to write an equation for each subtraction problem.

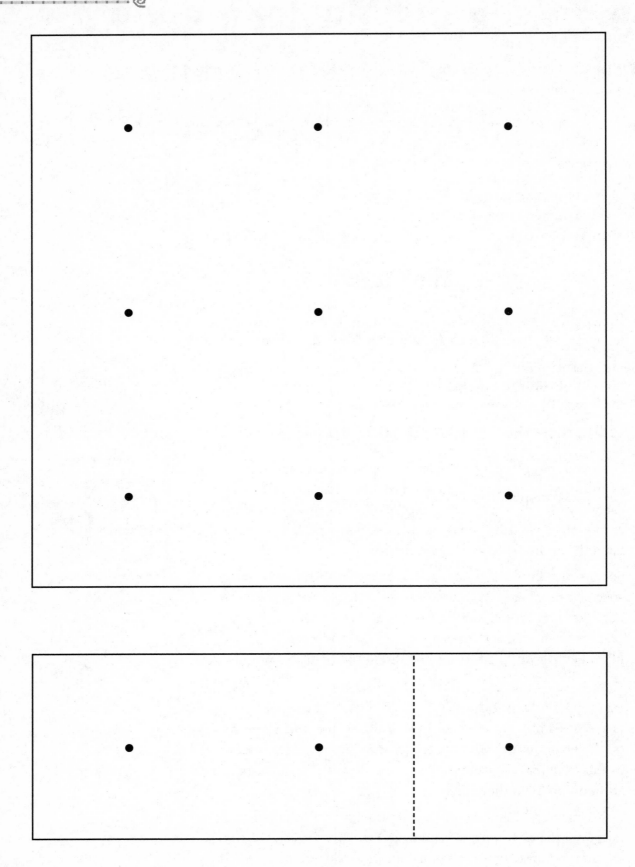

Clip-On Petal Counters

Students' math skills will bloom with these special flower counters.

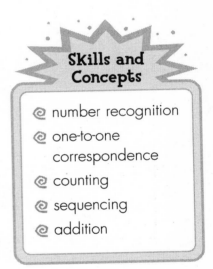

Materials

- 11 6-inch plastic plates in a light color
- black fine-point permanent marker
- wipe-off marker
- 55 plastic spring-type clothespins in a variety of colors

Making the Clip-On Petal Counters

1 Use a permanent marker to label the bottom of each plate with a numeral from 0 to 10.

2 Turn each plate over. Use the permanent marker to draw a corresponding number of dots along the plate rim, spacing the dots evenly around the rim.

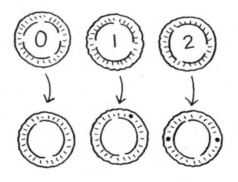

3 If desired, use a wipe-off marker to write on the top of each plate a simple equation or number word that corresponds to the numeral on the bottom of the plate.

4 To use, children attach one clothespin petal to each dot and then count all the "petals" on the flower.

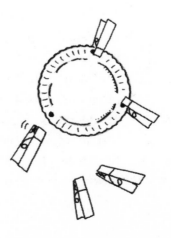

Skills and Concepts

- number recognition
- one-to-one correspondence
- counting
- sequencing
- addition

HANDY HINTS

▲ If plastic clothespins are not available, you might spray-paint wooden clothespins in several different colors. (Use nontoxic paint.) Allow the paint to dry thoroughly before use.

▲ If desired, substitute 6-inch posterboard circles for the plates. Label one side of each circle with a numeral and the other with the corresponding number of dots. Then laminate the circles for durability.

▲ If you want students to work with larger numerals, label an additional set of plates from 11 to 21, as described on page 11. For the entire set of plates (0 to 21), you will need 231 colored clothespins.

Ways to Use the Clip-On Petal Counters

◆ Ask children to attach one clothespin petal to each dot on the paper plate flower. Have them count the petals as they add each one to the flower. When finished, instruct children to refer to the back of the flower to check their answers.

◆ After children place the petals on all of their flowers, challenge them to arrange the flowers in numerical order. Have them check their work by turning over the plates and comparing their sequence to a number line.

◆ Use a wipe-off marker to write the corresponding number word on the top of each plate. Have children read the word, clip on the appropriate number of petals, and then check their work by looking at the numeral on the plate bottom.

◆ For practice in simple addition, use a wipe-off marker to write a simple equation on the top of each plate. The sum of the addition problem should equal the numeral on the bottom of the plate. Then ask children to attach clothespins of one color for the first addend and another color for the second. After they find the sum, have children look at the bottom of each plate to check their answers.

Glitter Concept Gloves

These glittery gloves will help children sparkle with basic number knowledge.

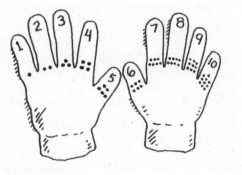

Materials

- 1 pair of white or light-colored cotton work gloves (small adult size works best)
- blue, red, and green glitter fabric pens

Making the Glitter Concept Gloves

1 Place the gloves palms-down on a table, with the thumbs side by side.

2 Use the blue glitter pen to write the numeral 1 at the top of the little finger of the left glove. Then write the numerals 2 through 10 in sequence on the other fingers, ending with 10 on the little finger of the right glove.

3 With the red glitter pen, draw a set of dots at the base of each finger to correspond to the numeral on the fingertip.

4 Starting with the little finger of the left glove, fold each finger back onto the glove. Use the green glitter pen to write the number word for the corresponding numeral along the length of each folded finger.

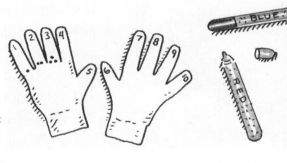

Skills and Concepts

- number recognition
- counting
- number words
- addition

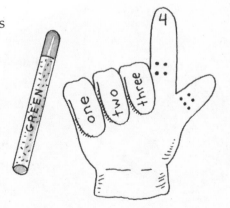

HANDY HINTS

▲ To make a simpler version, draw the dot pattern on each glove finger, then write the corresponding numeral on the palm side of

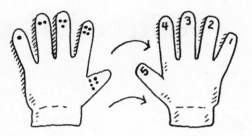

the finger. Similarly, you can write a number word on each finger and the corresponding numeral on the palm side (or the reverse).

▲ For a variation, you might write the ordinal number (first, second, third, and so on) on the palm side of each finger instead of the number word.

▲ According to each child's (or your) preference, the concept gloves can be worn while in use or placed on a flat surface in front of the child.

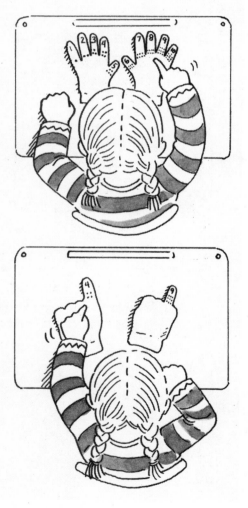

Ways to Use the Glitter Concept Gloves

◆ Invite children to use the concept gloves to practice counting. Children can look at the numerals as they count, or fold the fingertips under the glove and count by the dots at the base of each finger.

◆ To provide practice in number recognition, call out a number and have children find it on the gloves. Alternatively, fold the fingers back on the gloves, then ask children to find the corresponding number word.

◆ Have children use the concept gloves to identify specific numbers according to their position in a sequence. For instance, you might ask students to tell which number comes after 5 or before 7.

◆ For addition, place the gloves palms-down on a table. Then call out a simple addition problem. Have children fold all the fingers under the gloves except the two with numerals from the problem. Ask students to count the dots on the remaining extended fingers to find the sum.

Hex-Nut Counting Stairs

Children will go nuts over this tactile counting board.

Materials

- counting stairs pattern, page 17
- tape
- nail
- hammer
- 1-foot length of 2- by 4-inch wood
- power drill with $\frac{3}{8}$-inch drill bit
- 4-foot wooden dowel, $\frac{3}{8}$-inch in diameter
- coping saw
- wood glue
- 55 hexagonal nuts with $\frac{1}{2}$-inch hole
- fine-grade sandpaper
- $\frac{1}{2}$-inch (or $\frac{3}{4}$-inch) self-adhesive vinyl numerals

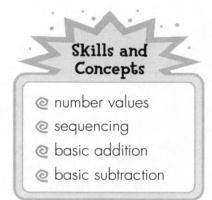

Skills and Concepts

- number values
- sequencing
- basic addition
- basic subtraction

Making the Hex-Nut Counting Stairs

1. Cut apart the patterns and tape them together where indicated. Tape the pattern strip to the board. To mark each hole in the board, use a hammer to tap a nail into the board at each dot. Make sure you remove the nail each time. After all the holes have been marked, remove the pattern.

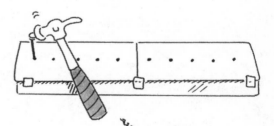

2. Drill a $\frac{3}{8}$-inch hole at each mark, drilling each hole about $1\frac{1}{2}$ inches deep.

3. Use the saw to cut the dowel into 10 lengths. Start by cutting a $2\frac{1}{2}$-inch length, then a 3-inch length. Cut each consecutive length $\frac{1}{2}$ inch longer than the one before. When finished, you will have 10 dowels with lengths of $2\frac{1}{2}$ inches to 7 inches (with $\frac{1}{2}$-inch left over).

4. Glue each dowel into a hole, starting with the shortest at one end of the board and finishing with the longest at the other end. Use a generous amount of wood glue, and press each dowel firmly into the hole. Wipe off any excess glue, then allow the glue to dry thoroughly (one to two days).

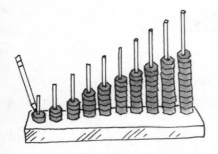

5 After the glue dries, place one nut on the shortest dowel, two nuts on the next dowel, and so on, until you have 10 nuts on the last dowel. Use a pencil to mark the top of each stack of nuts on the dowel (each dowel will extend beyond its stack of nuts).

6 Then remove the nuts and carefully saw off the top of each dowel at the mark.

7 Sand the board and dowels to smooth the surface and edges.

8 Affix the numerals 1 to 10 to the board.

HANDY HINTS

▲ If self-adhesive numerals are not available, use a black permanent marker to write (or stencil) the numerals directly on the board.

▲ If desired, spray-paint the board with a bright color of spray enamel after you sand it. Then add the numerals to the board.

Ways to Use the Hex-Nut Counting Stairs

◆ To teach about number values, have a child fit as many nuts onto each dowel as possible. Explain that this is the quantity of nuts equal to the numeral shown on the board. Then empty the board and ask the child to count out a specific quantity of nuts. To check his or her work, have the child place the counted nuts onto the corresponding dowel. If the top nut is level with the top of the dowel, the student counted correctly.

◆ Ask children to count out sets of nuts from 1 to 10, and then sequence the sets on the board. If sequenced correctly, the stacked nuts will form a "staircase." For an alternative, have students count out a series of number sets, such as 4, 5, and 6, to sequence on the board.

◆ Fill the board with hex nuts, then present children with a simple addition problem. Ask them to remove the nuts from the dowels that correspond to the numbers in the problem. Have them count the removed nuts to find the sum.

◆ To help children understand basic subtraction, give them the empty board, then present a simple equation. To solve, students fill the dowel corresponding to the larger number with nuts. Then they remove the smaller number and count the remaining nuts on the dowel to find the answer.

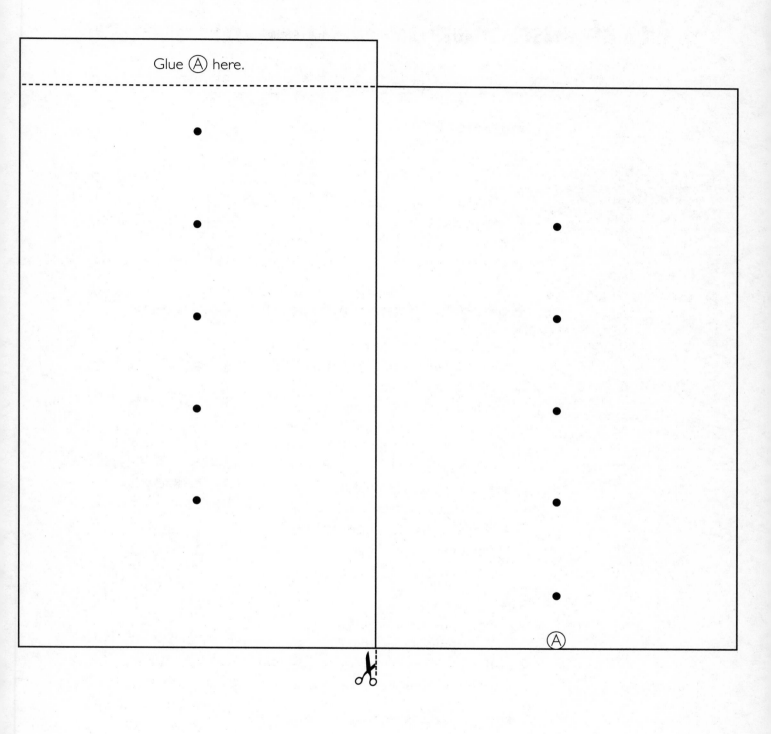

Glue Ⓐ here.

Ⓐ

Mathville Paper Bag Community

Basic math concepts are in the bag with this creative community.

Materials

- 11 plain brown paper grocery bags
- colored markers
- yellow construction paper
- scissors
- glue

Making the Mathville Paper Bag Community

1. Use the markers to draw an outline of a different community building—such as a fire station, hospital, school, fast-food restaurant, or house—on the front of each bag. For each of 10 buildings, cut out and glue on yellow construction-paper windows to the front, making sure that each bag contains a different numeral, from 1 to 10. Omit a window altogether on the eleventh bag.

2. Add a front door to each building, and draw other details as desired. Be creative, but also make sure that the windows are easily distinguished from the other building details.

3. Turn each bag over and draw a back door. On this door write the numeral for the number of windows on the front of the building. When finished, you will have 11 buildings labeled with 0 to 10.

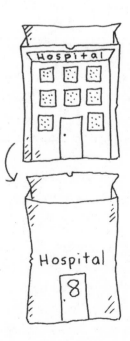

HANDY HINTS

▲ If desired, create a paper bag community of 21 bags to represent numerals from 0 to 20.

▲ Rather than label the back doors with numerals, you might label them with number words.

▲ Involve students in making the paper bag buildings. Simply assign a different number to each child, then ask the child to create a building with the assigned number of windows.

▲ For sturdier buildings, you might use plain cardboard boxes instead of paper bags.

Ways to Use the Mathville Paper Bag Community

◆ To use, have children count the number of windows on each building and then look at the back door to check their answers. As an alternative, have children write their counting results for each building on a sticky note to attach to the front door. Then they can compare the numerals on their sticky notes to the numerals on the back of the bags.

◆ Line up the paper bag buildings in random order. Challenge small groups of children to find the building with a specified number of windows. The first child to find the correct building can call out the number for the next round of play.

◆ Invite children to line up the buildings, sequencing them by the number of windows. To extend this activity, have students sort the bags by odd and even numbers of windows. Then have them sequence the two sets of buildings along an imaginary street, with buildings representing even numbers on one side and buildings representing odd numbers on the other.

◆ Provide children with a supply of dolls, plush animals, and toy figures. Have children select a building and then fill the bag with the number of "occupants" that corresponds to the label on the back door. For example, children will place four occupants in the building labeled "4."

Ten-Count Pegboard

Reinforce early math concepts with the visual and tactile experiences provided by this unique pegboard.

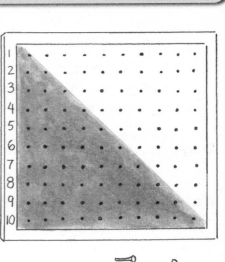

Skills and Concepts

- ℮ counting
- ℮ number words
- ℮ basic facts to 10
- ℮ missing addends

Materials

- ■ 1 square foot of a $\frac{1}{4}$-inch pegboard sheet (with 12 rows and 12 columns of holes)
- ■ 4 $1\frac{1}{2}$- by $2\frac{1}{8}$-inch wood spools (available at craft stores)
- ■ wood glue
- ■ masking tape
- ■ tagboard
- ■ spray paint in a bright color
- ■ yellow vinyl tape
- ■ $\frac{1}{2}$-inch black self-adhesive vinyl numerals (1–10)
- ■ 55 golf tees

Making the Ten-Count Pegboard

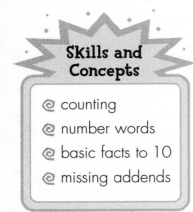

1 To attach feet to the pegboard, glue the flat end of a spool under each corner of the board. Allow the glue to dry.

2 Cover the line of holes along each edge with masking tape.

3 Cut a tagboard triangle large enough to cover half the pegboard, as shown. Tape the triangle over the upper right corner of the pegboard, leaving one hole exposed in the top row, two in the second row, and so on, with 10 holes exposed on the bottom row.

4 Spray a coat of paint over the exposed area of the pegboard. After the paint dries, apply a second coat if needed.

5 When thoroughly dry, remove the tagboard triangle and masking tape.

6 Carefully cover the line of holes along each edge of the pegboard with vinyl tape.

7 Affix a self-adhesive numeral, from 1 to 10, to the left of each row on the board (the numerals can be placed on the vinyl tape).

HANDY HINTS

▲ Instead of self-adhesive numerals, write (or stencil) the numerals directly onto the board with a permanent marker.

▲ If children have difficulty understanding how to use the painted area of the board as a visual guide, temporarily mask the additional holes on the unpainted section with a tagboard triangle. Once students understand how to use the masked board, remove the triangle and have children use only the visual guide.

Ways to Use the Ten-Count Pegboard

◆ To practice counting, children count out and insert the corresponding number of golf tees into the row for each numeral. Students check their work by making sure each tee is in a hole on the painted section of the board.

◆ For practice in number word identification, program each of 10 notecards with a numeral from 1 to 10. Write the corresponding number word on the back of each card. Stack the cards with the number words faceup. To use, a child draws a card, counts the number of tees corresponding to the number word on the card, and places them in the appropriate row on the pegboard. To check his or her answer, the child compares the numeral on the card to the numeral for the row on the pegboard.

◆ Give children golf tees in two colors to practice addition facts to 10. Have them use the two tee colors to create sets that can be combined to equal a given number. For example, 1 white tee plus 4 red tees equals 5, and 2 white tees plus 3 red tees also equals 5. To check their work, children insert each combination of tees in the row for the given number to make sure the sets add up.

◆ Challenge children to solve missing addend problems. Present a problem, such as 3 + _ = 7. To solve, a child places three tees in the row for 7. The child then determines how many more tees are needed to complete the row.

◆ Present children with simple subtraction problems to solve. To begin, children fill the row for the larger number (minuend) with tees. Then they subtract, or remove, the number of tees indicated in the problem (the subtrahend) and count the remaining tees to find the answer.

Count 'n' Cliposaurus

Children can learn about number values, addition, and more with this prehistoric pal.

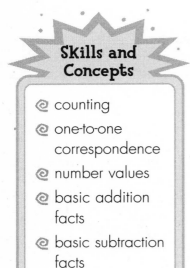
Materials

- cliposaurus pattern, page 24
- posterboard
- marker in any color of your choice
- glue
- scissors
- black fine-point permanent marker
- laminator
- plastic clothespins (2 colors)

Making the Count 'n' Cliposaurus

1 Enlarge and color the cliposaurus pattern.

2 Glue the pattern to posterboard. Once the glue is dry, cut out the shape.

3 Beginning at the neck and ending at the tail, draw 10 dots along the top edge of the cliposaurus's back (or draw 18 dots if you plan to use the counter for all of the basic addition and subtraction facts).

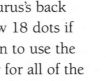

4 Laminate the cliposaurus for durability.

5 Use the black permanent marker to write each numeral from 1 to 10 (or 1 to 18) on a separate clothespin.

HANDY HINTS

▲ As an alternative for your early learners, you might make ten cliposauruses. Draw a different quantity of dots on each one, from 1 to 10, then label the back of each with the corresponding numeral (and/or number word). To use, children simply count and clip an unmarked clothespin "dinosaur plate" onto each dot on a cliposaurus.

▲ If desired, invite each child to create and name his or her own count 'n' cliposaurus.

Ways to Use the Count 'n' Cliposaurus

◆ To use, children count out a designated number of clothespins. Then they clip each plate, in sequence from left to right, onto a dot on the cliposaurus. Have students use a number line to check their work.

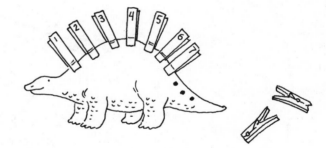

◆ Give children basic addition facts to solve with the count 'n' cliposaurus. First, present a problem, such as "3 + 5." To find the answer, children count out a different-colored set of unmarked clothespins for each addend. Then they clip the plates onto the cliposaurus and count the total. Have them check their answers against a number line.

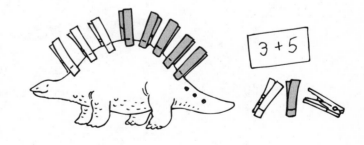

◆ Present children with basic facts in subtraction. To solve, have them count out the number of clothespin plates for the larger number in the equation to clip onto the cliposaurus. Then have them subtract by removing plates equal to the smaller number. Instruct children to use a number line to check their answers.

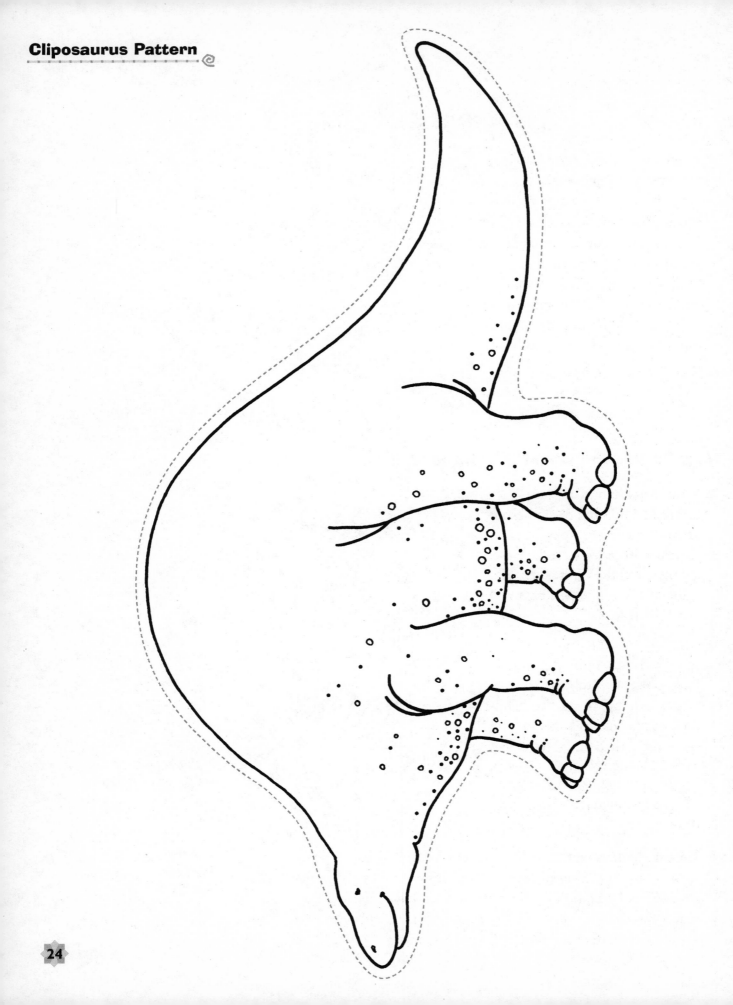

Dinosaur Eggs

Hatch some "eggs-traordinary" number learning fun with these versatile dinosaur eggs.

Materials

- 1 dozen large plastic eggs
- 55 mini dinosaur stickers
- 55 mini dinosaur counters
- black fine-point permanent marker
- large shoe box lined with shredded paper

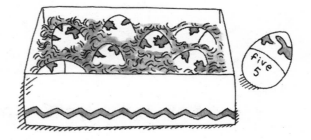

Making the Dinosaur Eggs

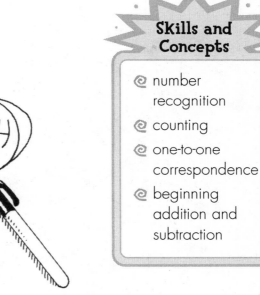

1 Using the permanent marker, label the short, wider end of 11 eggs with a numeral from 0 to 10. (You might also want to write the number word around the barrel of the egg.) Then open each egg and write the same numeral on the inside of the tall, narrow end of the egg.

2 On the outside of the tall, narrow end of each egg, attach the number of dinosaur stickers corresponding to the numeral written inside.

3 Fill each egg with the corresponding number of dinosaurs, then close the egg.

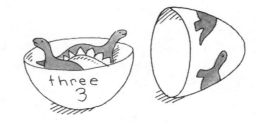

4 Put a few extra dinosaurs in the unmarked egg. These can be used as replacements for any lost or damaged dinosaurs.

5 Place all the eggs and dinosaurs in the shoe box "nest."

> ### Skills and Concepts
> - number recognition
> - counting
> - one-to-one correspondence
> - beginning addition and subtraction

HANDY HINTS

▲ Mini dinosaur counters can be purchased from school supply vendors, such as ETA Cuisenaire, **www.etacuisenaire.com**.

▲ If desired, decorate the shoe box with plastic adhesive covering and dinosaur stickers.

▲ Use small plastic eggs as an alternative to the larger eggs. Fill the eggs with beans instead of mini dinosaurs.

Ways to Use the Dinosaur Eggs

◆ To provide counting practice, have children open each egg and count the dinosaur contents. Reinforce one-to-one correspondence by asking them to make sure there is one dinosaur for every sticker on the egg.

◆ Empty the eggs, placing all the dinosaurs in a pile. Then place the egg halves on a table so that the numerals and dinosaur stickers are easily visible. To use, children match each dinosaur-labeled egg half to its corresponding numbered half. They then check their work by comparing the numeral on the outside to the numeral inside the egg. Finally, they fill each egg with the appropriate number of dinosaurs and place the egg in the nest.

◆ Use your dinosaur eggs to teach beginning addition and subtraction skills. To add two numbers, children simply empty the contents of the two eggs and then count the total number of dinosaurs. To subtract, they empty the contents of the egg corresponding to the larger number in the problem. Then they subtract the given number of dinosaurs and count the remaining ones to arrive at the answer.

T-rex Number Track

Invite children to trek with Tyrannosaurus rex across this prehistoric number line.

Materials

- T-rex footprint and dinosaur patterns, page 29
- tagboard
- scissors
- brown and green plastic adhesive covering (or two contrasting colors or your choice)
- pencil
- 2- by 10-foot length of clear plastic sheeting, at least 6 mil thick (available at home-improvement stores)
- yardstick
- permanent marker
- 4-inch black self-adhesive vinyl numerals (1–10)

Making the T-rex Number Track

1 To make tracers, outline the T-rex footprint and dinosaur patterns on tagboard. Cut out the resulting shapes.

2 Use the pencil to trace 12 footprints onto the brown plastic adhesive covering and 55 dinosaurs onto the green covering. Cut out each shape. (See Handy Hints for a quick way to cut out these shapes.)

3 Spread out the plastic sheeting. Divide the length of sheeting into 11 equal sections (each will be about 11 inches long) by marking the edge with a permanent marker.

4 Starting at one end of the sheeting, affix the vinyl 0 in the first marked section along the right side. Remove the backing from two footprints and carefully affix these side by side next to the numeral.

5 In the next section, affix the vinyl 1 and one footprint, as in step 4. Make this a right footprint. Then affix one dinosaur to the left of the footprint.

6 Prepare each consecutive section as described in step 5, placing the numerals and corresponding number of dinosaurs in sequential order up to 10. Alternate right and left footprints.

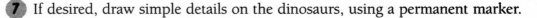

7 If desired, draw simple details on the dinosaurs, using a permanent marker.

8 To use, spread out the number track on the floor. When not in use, roll it up and secure the roll with a rubber band.

HANDY HINTS

▲ For a quick way to cut out the patterns, cut the brown plastic covering into 12 5- by 7-inch rectangles. Stack several rectangles together, trace the footprint on the top one, and staple around it. Cut out the shape through all thicknesses. For the dinosaurs, use 55 4-inch squares of the green plastic covering.

▲ If 4-inch vinyl numerals are not available, trace the numeral patterns on pages 111 to 112 of this book onto a solid color of plastic covering and cut them out. (If desired, enlarge the numerals first.)

▲ If desired, double the length of the plastic sheeting and extend the number track to 20. Reduce the patterns and cut out 22 footprints and 220 dinosaurs for the extended track.

▲ Use the same materials to create a wall number line similar to the one shown.

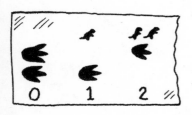

Ways to Use the T-rex Number Track

◆ To reinforce counting and one-to-one correspondence, have a child step on each footprint, name the numeral, then count out the corresponding number of dinosaurs on the track. Or give the child a basket of dinosaur counters and have him or her place a counter on each dinosaur.

◆ For practice in number sequences, ask a child to step on the footprint of a specific number. Then have the child name the number before or after that number. Or name a sequence of three numbers, leaving out one number. Ask the child to step on the footprint of the missing number.

◆ To incorporate movement, ask a child to step onto the footprint for each odd number in sequence, naming each number as he or she lands on it. Have the child repeat for even numbers. To provide a visual cue for this activity, tape a light-colored sheet of construction paper behind each odd or even number on the number track.

◆ For simple addition, call out an equation with a sum of up to 10. Have a child step on the footprint representing the numeral for the first addend. Then have him or her walk forward the number of footprints equal to the second addend. The numeral of the footprint the child stops on should represent the answer.

Daisy Counting Garden

Pick this garden full of daisies to give children practice in a variety of number concepts.

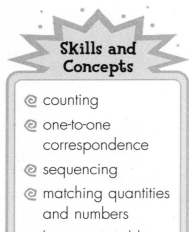

Materials

- 11 plastic or silk daisies with stems
- scissors
- $\frac{3}{4}$-inch-wide green vinyl tape
- black fine-point permanent marker
- large block of floral foam

Making the Daisy Counting Garden

1 Use scissors to cut petals off of one flower, leaving 10 evenly spaced petals around the flower center. Then repeat with another flower, this time leaving nine petals. Continue in this manner, creating a flower with one less petal each time. There will be no petals left around the center of the last flower.

2 Cut a 2-inch length of green tape for each flower. Fold the tape over the middle of the flower stem and press the sticky sides together to create a "leaf." Trim the tape into a leaf shape.

3 Use the permanent marker to label each leaf with the corresponding number of flower petals. If desired, write the number word on the back of the leaf.

4 Poke each flower stem into the floral foam to create a daisy garden.

Skills and Concepts

- counting
- one-to-one correspondence
- sequencing
- matching quantities and numbers
- beginning addition

HANDY HINTS

▲ If desired, include an additional 10 flowers—with petal amounts from 11 to 20—in your garden.

▲ For variety, you may wish to use an assortment of flowers. If you do, make sure you prepare a flower to represent each number from 0 to 11 (or 20, if you plan to work with higher numbers).

▲ Keep the extra petals for additional activities. For instance, children can count out loose petals to match the number on each flower. Or they can use them as counters for simple addition and subtraction problems.

Ways to Use the Daisy Counting Garden

◆ Place the flowers in the foam block with numerals facing away from children. Then invite them to pick one flower at a time from the garden. Have them count the petals on each flower and check their answers by looking at the numeral (or number word) on the tape leaf.

◆ Call out a specific number from 1 to 10. Ask children to search the garden for the daisy with the corresponding number. When they find it, have them pick the flower, count its petals, and check the numeral on the leaf to see if they picked the right daisy.

◆ Give children the empty block of floral foam and the daisies. Challenge them to count the petals and "plant" the daisies in the garden in numerical order. Have them check their work by comparing the sequence of numerals on the leaves to a number line.

◆ Ask children to pick two daisies from the garden and use the petal count of the flowers to create an addition problem. For example, their equation might be "4 petals + 7 petals = ___." Then have students count the total number of petals on the two flowers to arrive at the answer.

Cool Cup 'n' Straw Counters

These special straw counters are a refreshing way to teach children basic number concepts.

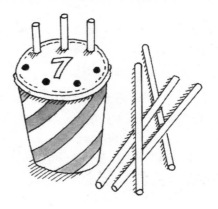

Materials

- 11 plastic cups with soft plastic snap-on lids
- hole punch
- tape
- 1-inch self-adhesive vinyl numerals (0–10)
- 55 plastic straws, in two colors

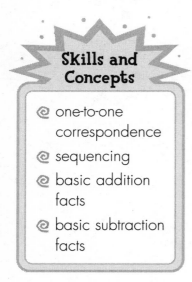

Skills and Concepts

- one-to-one correspondence
- sequencing
- basic addition facts
- basic subtraction facts

Making the Cool Cup 'n' Straw Counters

1. Carefully slip a hole punch over the rim of each of 10 cup lids. Then punch the desired number of holes, from 1 to 10, in each lid. (Be sure to include any existing straw holes in your hole count. If the hole is in the center, tape it closed from the bottom of the lid and cover the space with a numeral, as indicated in step 2.)

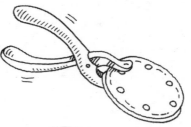

2. If the eleventh lid has a hole in it, cover the hole with tape.

3. Label each lid with a vinyl numeral corresponding to the number of holes in the lid.

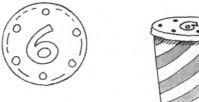

4. Snap a lid onto each cup.

HANDY HINTS

▲ Many restaurants provide complimentary plastic cups and lids with their kids' meals. You might request a donation of cups and lids from a local restaurant.

▲ In addition to labeling each lid with a numeral, you may also wish to write the number word on the lid.

▲ Instead of using vinyl numerals, you might stencil or simply write numerals on the lids with a black permanent marker.

▲ For larger numbers, use 19 cup and lid sets, punching from 1 to 18 holes in each of 18 lids (18 holes fit nicely on a $3\frac{1}{2}$-inch lid). You will need 231 straws for the 19 cup 'n' straw counters.

Ways to Use the Cool Cup 'n' Straw Counters

◆ To use, children place a straw in each hole in the cup lids. Once the holes have been filled, have children count the straws in each lid. To check their answers, have them compare their counting results to the numeral on the lid.

◆ For sequencing practice, have children fill each cup lid with straws. Then instruct them to put the cups in numerical sequence. To extend, ask children to sequence a set of up to five cup 'n' straw counters that are presented in random order. Or present a series of counters, leaving one out of the sequence. Challenge children to fill in the missing cup.

◆ Present children with simple addition problems. To solve, have them use two different straw colors to fill the cups for each addend. Then have them add the two straw sets together. To check their work, children can remove the straws from the addend cups and insert them into the cup representing their answer. If the straws fill all the holes in the answer cup, then their answer is correct. To extend, challenge children to use the counters to create different addend sets that equal a given sum. Or use the cups to set up missing addend problems for children to solve.

◆ To solve simple subtraction problems, have children fill the cup that represents the larger number with straws. Then have them remove the number of straws corresponding to the smaller number. Ask them to count the remaining straws to solve the problem. For example, for "5 − 2," students fill the "5" cup with straws. They then remove two straws and count the remaining straws to arrive at the answer of 3.

Stepping Stones

Use these inexpensive, durable number squares to help children step into successful math learning.

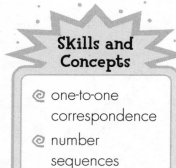

Materials

- footprint patterns, page 36
- tagboard
- scissors
- pencil
- plastic adhesive covering in a dark color
- 21 12-inch-square linoleum tiles in a solid light color
- 4-inch black self-adhesive vinyl numerals (0–20)
- sticker dots in two colors
- carpet tape

Skills and Concepts

- one-to-one correspondence
- number sequences
- odd and even numbers
- simple addition and subtraction

Making the Stepping Stones

1. To make tracers, outline the two footprint patterns on tagboard. Cut out the shapes.

2. With the pencil, trace 11 of each footprint onto the plastic adhesive covering. Cut out each footprint.

3. Affix the vinyl 0 along the lower right side of a tile. Remove the backing from two footprints and carefully affix these side by side to the left of the numeral.

4. On the next tile, affix the 1 to the lower right and a right footprint to the left, as in step 3. Then affix one color dot above the number. On another tile, similarly attach the vinyl 2, a left footprint, and two dots in a different color above the number.

5. Prepare each consecutive tile, up to 20, as described in step 4, alternating the two footprints and colors so that tiles with odd numbers have right footprints and dots of the same color and even-number tiles have left footprints and dots of a second color.

6. To use, lay the tiles on the floor in numerical order, securing them to the floor with carpet tape.

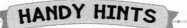

HANDY HINTS

▲ If you use self-adhesive tiles, you can fold away a little of the backing at opposite corners and stick the tile to the floor. When finished, pull the tile up and fold the backing over the exposed adhesive.

▲ To extend the "life" of the footprints, numerals, and dots on the tiles, have children walk on the stepping stones in soft-sole shoes or in socks.

▲ If 4-inch vinyl numerals are not available, you can trace the numeral patterns on pages 111 to 112 of this book onto a solid color of plastic adhesive covering, then cut them out to use on your stepping stones. (If desired, enlarge the numerals first.)

Ways to Use the Stepping Stones

◆ Reinforce counting and one-to-one correspondence with your stepping stones. Starting at "0," have a child step on each stone, name the numeral, then count out the corresponding dots on the stone. If desired, you can give the child a basket of bear counters and have him or her place a counter on each dot.

◆ To practice number sequences, give a child a set of tiles to put in numerical order. Or instruct a child to stand on the stone for a specific number and then name the number before or after that number. You can also present a child with a sequence of several numbers, leaving out one number. Ask the child to step on the stone of the missing number.

◆ Ask a child to hop onto the odd-number stones, naming the numbers as he or she lands on them. Have the child repeat for even numbers. As the child performs this activity, encourage him or her to use the visual cues provided by the different footprints and color dots on the tiles.

◆ For simple addition, call out an equation with a sum of up to 20. Have a child stand on the stone corresponding to the first addend. To solve the problem, ask the child to step forward the number of stones equal to the second addend. The stone on which the child stops should contain the answer. For subtraction, the child stands on the stone representing the larger number in the equation. Then he or she steps backward the number of stones equal to the smaller number to find the answer.

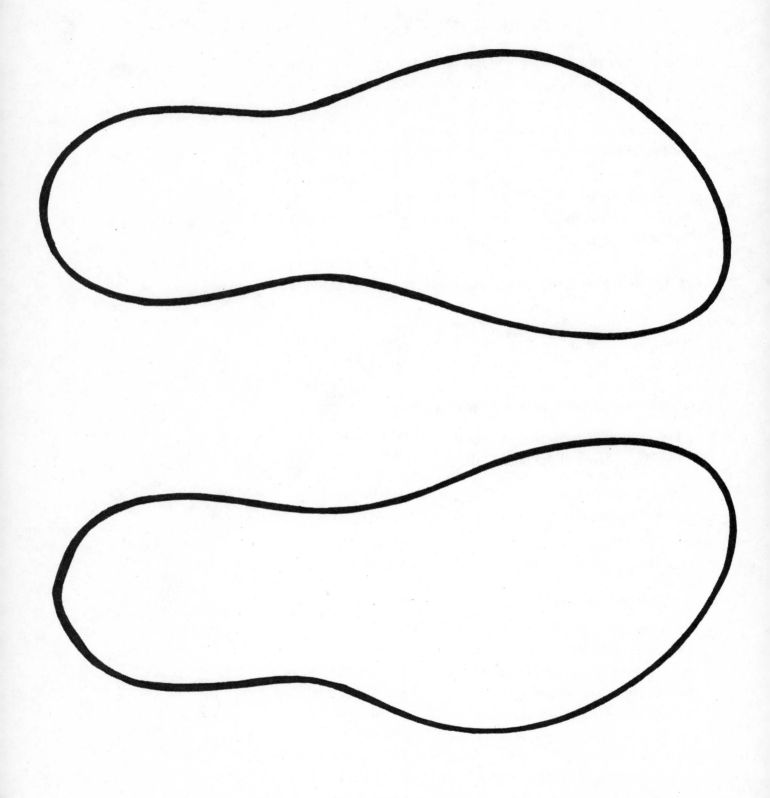

Perfect 100s Pegboard

This pegboard is the perfect tool for counting to 100 and practicing a variety of other math skills.

Materials

- square foot of $\frac{1}{4}$-inch peg board sheet (with 12 rows and 12 columns of holes)
- 4 $1\frac{1}{2}$- by $2\frac{1}{2}$-inch wood spools (available in craft stores)
- wood glue
- masking tape
- spray paint in a bright color
- yellow vinyl tape
- black fine-tip permanent marker
- two sets of 100 golf tees, each set in a different color

Skills and Concepts

- counting to 100
- place value
- addition and subtraction
- skip-counting

Making the Perfect 100s Pegboard

1 To attach feet to the pegboard, glue the flat end of a spool under each corner of the board. Allow the glue to dry.

2 Cover the line of holes along each edge of the pegboard with masking tape so that only 100 holes remain exposed.

3 Spray a coat of paint over the exposed area of the pegboard. After the paint dries, apply a second coat if needed.

4 When thoroughly dry, replace the masking tape with vinyl tape.

5 Carefully affix a length of vinyl tape under each row of holes. Use the permanent marker to write a numeral on the tape under each hole, starting with "1" at the top left and ending with "100" at the bottom right.

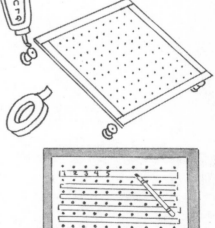

HANDY HINTS

▲ If you wish to use your pegboard for graphing, remove the vinyl tape under each line of holes. Attach a graph label at the top of each column of holes (such as color names to graph students' favorite colors). Then have children place tees in the appropriate columns to create a graph.

Ways to Use the Perfect 100s Pegboard

◆ To practice counting, children count out a given number of tees, up to 100. Then they insert the tees into the holes to check their counting for accuracy.

◆ For practice in place value, fill in tees on the board up to a specified number. Ask children to use the columns and rows to help them report the number in tens and ones. Or prepare cards with numerals written as sets of tens and ones. Have children fill in tees on the board to represent the numerals on the cards.

◆ To practice adding sums to 100, present children with a problem. Then instruct them to use different tee colors to create a set for each addend. Have them insert the two sets of tees into the board to find the sum. For example, for "36 + 21," children put 36 white tees and 21 red tees into the board to get the sum of "57."

◆ Present children with subtraction problems to solve on the pegboard. To begin, children fill the holes for the larger number with tees. Then they subtract, or remove, the number of tees for the smaller number and count the remaining tees in the row to find the answer.

◆ For skip-counting, have children use a different-colored tee for every number in the skip-count sequence. For example, they can fill in the board with white tees and then substitute a red tee for every multiple of five. To skip-count, children name the numbers, in sequence, that are identified by the different-colored tee.

Zip & Skip Number Line

> With these unique counters, children can zip right through basic counting concepts.

Materials

- 2 20-inch zippers in a light color
- ruler
- black ultra-fine-point permanent marker

Making the Zip & Skip Number Line

1 Working from the bottom to the top of the zipper (not the zipper tape), measure and mark one-inch intervals on the zipper tape along the length of the zipper. You will make 20 marks, with the last one falling at the top of the zipper.

2 Label the bottom end of the zipper "0." Then label the first mark "5," and each consecutive mark with a multiple of five, ending with "100" at the top mark.

3 To make a 10s skip-counting line, measure and mark the zipper tape at 2-inch intervals. Then label the zipper from 0 to 100 in multiples of ten.

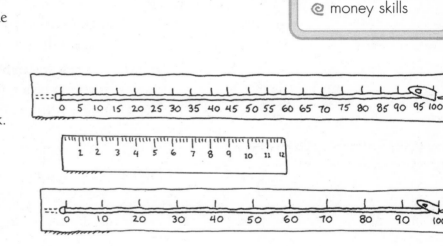

Skills and Concepts

- skip-counting
- sequencing
- number values
- money skills

HANDY HINTS

▲ For durability and stability, mount the zippers on a fabric-covered piece of sturdy cardboard. To do this, squeeze a thin line of fabric glue along the edges of the zipper tape. Wipe away any excess glue, making sure it does not ooze onto the zipper teeth. Then carefully press the zipped zippers onto the fabric board. Allow the glue to dry thoroughly before using the zippers.

▲ If you prefer, you can label the zippers for vertical counting.

▲ You can also make 20-inch zipper skip-counting lines for multiples of 20 and 25 to help reinforce money skills. For a 20s skip-counting line, mark every four inches on the zipper tape, then label the zipper in multiples of 20 from 0 to 100. To make a 25s skip-counting line, mark the zipper every five inches and label it with multiples of 25 from 0 to 100.

▲ For variety, mark and label a 26-inch zipper with the letters of the alphabet. Use the zipper to reinforce ordinal numbers (first letter, second letter, and so on) and concepts such as before, after, and between.

Ways to Use the Zip & Skip Number Line

◆ To use the 5s skip-counting line, a child unzips the zipper to zero. Then he or she zips the zipper up to a given number, calling out each multiple of five as it is passed. The child uses the 10s skip-counting line in the same manner, counting out multiples of ten as he or she zips the zipper to the given number.

◆ Have children zip one of the counting lines to a given number. Then have them name the multiple that comes before and/or after that number.

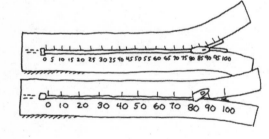

◆ With the 5s and 10s zipper skip-counting lines placed side by side, have children zip both to the same number (which will always be a multiple of ten). Then have students compare the counting lines to determine how many multiples of five are in the corresponding multiple of ten. Guide them to discover that the number of fives will be twice the number of tens.

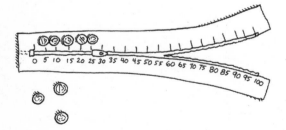

◆ To reinforce money skills, place a supply of real or play-money nickels with the 5s skip-counting lines. (If desired, you can use the patterns on page 88 to create the coins for this activity.) Next, present children with a multiple of five. Children will zip the zipper to the specified number and place a coin on each multiple along the zipped section of the zipper. Then they will count the coins to determine how many it takes to equal the money value of the given number. For example, for 25, children will zip the zipper to the 25 mark, place a nickel at every mark up to 25, then count the coins to discover that 5 nickels equals 25 cents. Children can also perform this activity using the 10s counting line and a supply of dimes.

Number Comparison Dino Puppet

This hungry dinosaur has an appetite for small and large numbers—and a variety of other math skills!

Materials

- dinosaur puppet patterns, page 43
- half-gallon milk carton, washed and dried
- pencil
- scissors
- tape
- craft knife
- green and red plastic adhesive covering
- large wiggle eyes
- craft glue
- white rickrack
- 5-inch square of tagboard
- dinosaur counters

Making the Number Comparison Dino Puppet

1. Cut off the top of the carton. Turn the carton over and use the bottom as the top for the puppet.

2. Cut out the carton pattern.

3. Fit the fold of the carton pattern over a corner of the carton and align the pointed ends with the top of the carton. Tape the pattern in place and trace it onto the carton. Use a craft knife and scissors to cut out the outlined section. Discard the removed piece.

4. Cover the outside of the carton with green plastic adhesive covering and the top with red plastic covering.

5. Fold up the cut section of the carton, as shown, to create a puppet head with a movable mouth. (The carton will fold naturally along an original seam.)

Skills and Concepts

- number comparisons
- ordinal numbers
- addition
- subtraction

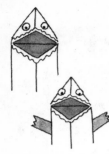

6 Glue on wiggle eyes. Glue rickrack teeth along the top and bottom edges of the mouth.

7 Cover the tagboard with green plastic covering. Trace the arm pattern twice onto the tagboard, then cut out the shapes. Glue an arm to each side of the puppet.

HANDY HINTS

▲ "Pop" bubbles in the plastic adhesive covering by poking them with a straight pin and pressing the air out.

▲ Add a craft-foam frill and other dinosaur details as desired.

▲ If desired, use dinosaur-shaped snacks instead of dinosaur counters.

▲ You may wish to decorate the puppet to resemble a dalmation (or other critter of your choice) instead of the dinosaur.

Ways to Use the Number Comparison Dino Puppet

◆ Provide children with practice in number comparisons. First, set up a story about a leaf-eating dinosaur that must select its lunch from one of two piles of leaves. On the chalkboard write the number of leaves in each pile. Then have children slip their hand inside the puppet and use their fingers and thumb to move its mouth. Invite them to use the puppet to identify and "eat" the larger number of leaves. Explain that when they point the puppet's open mouth toward the larger number, its shape creates a "greater than" sign.

◆ For learning about ordinal numbers, place 10 dinosaur counters in a row, leaving about two inches of space between each one. Ask a child to have the puppet "eat" the dinosaur counter in a specified position in the row, such as the fifth dinosaur.

◆ Have children use the puppet to arrange dinosaur counters into addend sets that represent a simple addition problem. They may wish to put each addend set on a separate paper plate and then have the puppet "eat" from each plate, counting the dinosaurs to find out how many are eaten all together. Alternatively, for subtraction, children can use the puppet to eat the number of counters equal to the smaller number in the problem. To find the answer, they simply count the remaining counters.

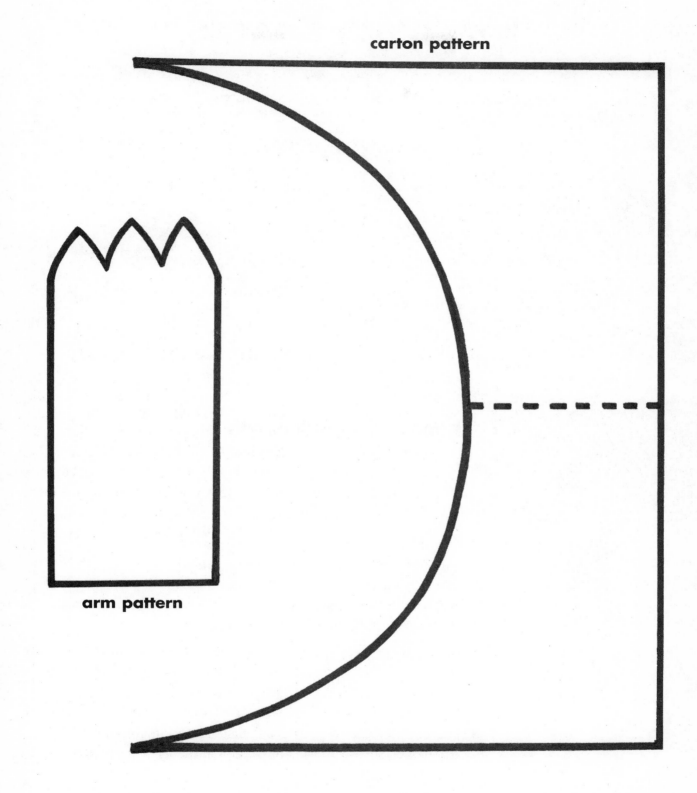

carton pattern

arm pattern

Mini Math Boards

Set aside the pencil and paper! These individual boards provide a fun, motivational way for children to practice math skills.

Materials

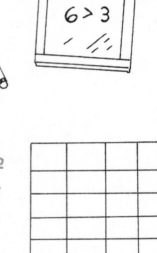

- sheet of white tile board (available in 4- by 8-foot sheets at home improvement stores)
- yardstick
- pencil
- hand or power saw
- medium- and fine-grade sandpaper
- wipe-off pens
- paper towels

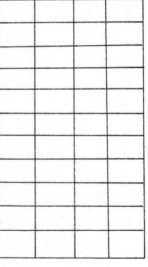

Skills and Concepts

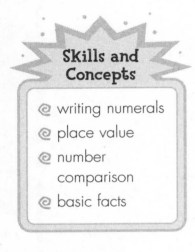

- writing numerals
- place value
- number comparison
- basic facts

Making the Mini Math Boards

1 Use the pencil and yardstick to mark the tile board in 48 8- by 12-inch rectangles. Or, if you prefer, mark the tile board in 32 12-inch squares. (You can measure both sizes horizontally or vertically since the measurements will be an exact fit either way.)

2 Carefully cut apart the rectangles with a hand or power saw.

3 Smooth the edges of each board first with the medium-grade sandpaper, then with the fine-grade sandpaper.

4 To use, children write their math solutions on the boards with a wipe-off pen. When ready, they erase the board clean with a paper towel.

HANDY HINTS

▲ If desired, cut a class quantity of 8- by 12-inch individual boards. Then measure and cut the remaining tile board into various sizes to be used as display boards or for group work.

▲ After cutting the tile board, you can sand each board just enough to remove any loose particles. Then edge each board with vinyl tape in the color of your choice.

▲ Provide wipe-off pens in different colors and tip styles, such as fine-point and chisel-tip. You may also wish to include scented markers for student use.

Ways to Use the Mini Math Boards

◆ Give each child an individual math board and wipe-off pen. Then call out a number. Have each child write the number on the board and hold it up to show his or her work. Alternatively, children can use their individual math boards to spell number words.

◆ To provide practice in place value, write a number on a math board and show it to children. Then instruct them to write the number in tens and ones on their boards. When children finish, write the correct combination on your own board to display to children. Have them check their work against yours. This activity can also be performed in reverse, where you write a number in values of tens and ones on your board. Then children write the corresponding numeral on their boards.

◆ Call out two numbers. Have children write the first number on the left side of their boards and the second number on the right. Then ask them to fill in the middle with a "greater than" or "less than" sign to compare the two numbers. Write the numbers with the correct sign on your own board to show children so that they can check their work.

◆ For practice in basic facts drill, call out an addition or subtraction fact to 18. Have children write the answer on their boards, and then hold the boards up to show their work. Later, children can use the boards in timed drill practice. Pairs of students can also use the boards in combination with flash cards to practice basic facts.

◆ Since these boards are so versatile, they can be used in many creative ways to teach math skills such as telling time, writing fractions, and identifying money.

Computation Cookies

Use these cookies for a yummy way to practice basic facts and operations.

Skills and Concepts

- addition
- subtraction
- multiplication
- division

Materials

- dough recipe (see step 1, below)
- large mixing bowl
- measuring cups
- spoon
- flour
- salt
- water
- food coloring
- waxed paper
- rolling pin
- cookie cutter
- magnetic tape
- steel cookie sheet

Making the Computation Cookies

1 Follow the recipe to make the dough cookies.

> ### DOUGH RECIPE
>
> Mix 1 cup salt and 4 cups flour in a bowl. Add food coloring to $1\frac{1}{2}$ cups water, then add the water to the dry mixture. Mix the ingredients until a firm dough forms. Knead the dough for five minutes, or until it has a uniform texture. Place the dough on waxed paper and roll it to about $\frac{1}{4}$-inch thick. Cut shapes from the dough with a cookie cutter. Set the cookies aside to air-dry (this may take a day or two, depending on the thickness of the cookies).

2 Attach a piece of magnetic tape to the back of each cookie. Make sure the magnet will support the weight of the cookie when it is placed on an upright magnetic surface.

3 Use the cookies on the cookie sheet to perform a variety of math functions.

HANDY HINTS

▲ Remind children that the dough cookies are not intended to be eaten. If desired, have children help you make the dough cookies and then a batch of real cookies. Ask them to compare the ingredients. Then invite children to enjoy the real cookies during snack time.

▲ For a quick-drying method, put the cookies on a foil-lined cookie sheet and set them in a 300°F oven for 1 to 2 hours. Be sure to check the cookies often, since drying time may vary depending on the size and thickness of the cookies.

▲ Before beginning, decide which skills you wish to reinforce with these manipulatives. Then make the appropriate quantity of cookies. For instance, you'll need 18 cookies for addition and subtraction facts and 81 for multiplication and division facts. Plan to make a few more cookies than you actually need, so that you'll have a supply of replacements for broken or lost cookies.

▲ If the cookie sheet is not large enough for operations requiring lots of cookies, use a magnetic board or the side of a file cabinet.

Ways to Use the Computation Cookies

◆ For addition facts, give children 18 cookies and the cookie sheet. Call out an addition problem. Have children count out the number of cookies for each addend and place them on the cookie sheet. Then have them count the total number of cookies to find the sum.

◆ To practice subtraction facts, children place the number of cookies equal to the larger number on the cookie sheet. Then they remove the number of cookies corresponding to the smaller number to find the answer.

◆ Present children with multiplication facts up to 81. Have them organize cookie sets on the cookie sheet to represent the multiplication problem. Then ask them to count (or multiply) the cookies to find the answer.

◆ Similarly, have children arrange cookies on the cookie sheet to represent problems for division facts. After they set up the "equations," ask children to use the cookies to find the answers.

Perky Pig Computer

Perk up math drill activities with this adorable pig computer.

Materials

- 3-quart plastic bleach or fabric-softener bottle with cap, thoroughly cleaned and dried and with label removed
- craft knife
- 4 corks, 1 to $1\frac{1}{2}$ inches tall and $\frac{3}{4}$ inch or more in diameter
- craft glue
- pink pipe cleaner
- pink felt
- scissors
- 2 large wiggle eyes or small styrofoam balls
- supply of 5- by 8-inch unlined index cards
- black and red fine-point permanent markers

Skills and Concepts

- addition
- subtraction
- multiplication
- division

Making the Perky Pig Computer

1 To make the pig's body, use the craft knife to cut a 1-inch by 3-inch slit approximately one inch behind the bottle's handle.

2 Turn the pig over and mark the placement of the pig's feet with a permanent marker. Make the marks for the front feet closer to the front of the body than the top slit. Use the craft knife to cut an X at each mark.

3 For the feet, push the narrow end of a cork into the pig body at each X. Glue each foot in place. Allow the glue to dry thoroughly.

4 Poke a hole in the pig's backside and push the pipe cleaner about one inch into the hole. Bend the end of the pipe cleaner inside the bottle and apply glue to secure it. On the outside of the body, twist the pipe cleaner around a marker to create a curly pig tail.

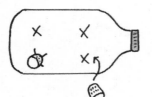

5 Cut out pig ears from the felt. Then glue on the ears and eyes. (For styrofoam ball eyes, draw pupils with the permanent marker.)

6 Use the black marker to write a "drill and practice" problem at the top of each index card. Write the answer at the bottom center of the card, using the red marker. Prepare a grade-level set of cards for basic facts in addition, subtraction, multiplication, and division.

7 Place the stack of cards in the top slit so that the problem on the front of card can be seen from the front of the pig.

HANDY HINTS

▲ When a card is inserted into the pig computer, make sure you can see the answer through the hole. If needed, cut the slit deeper, but be sure that the problem on each card remains visible above the pig's body.

▲ Paint the bottle with pink nontoxic spray enamel, if desired.

▲ Additional sets of cards can be created to provide practice in other math skills, such as comparing numbers, telling time, and identifying fractions and money.

▲ If preferred, decorate the bottle to resemble a dalmation, dinosaur, or other critter of your choice.

Ways to Use the Perky Pig Computer

◆ Place a set of fact cards in the pig computer. Have children answer each problem, remove the bottle cap "nose," and peek through the hole to see the correct answer (written in red) on the card. They might also write and solve each problem on paper. If desired, allow children to use pig counters to solve each problem.

◆ Invite pairs of children to use the computer in a game. To play, one child answers the problem on the computer card and the second child checks the answer. If the answer is correct, the child "oinks." If incorrect, he or she "squeals." The first child tries another answer for every problem that gets a "squeal."

◆ For group work, one child operates the computer by placing the cards in it and showing the other students the problem. Children write their answers on slips of paper (or they can use the mini math boards from page 44) and hold them up for the operator to see. The operator checks the computer for the answer, then signals children to let them know whether or not their answers are correct.

Monster Math-Muncher Machine

There's nothing scary about learning computation skills with this friendly monster fact machine.

Skills and Concepts

- ◉ addition
- ◉ subtraction
- ◉ multiplication
- ◉ division

Materials

- ▣ 2-quart milk or juice carton, thoroughly washed and dried
- ▣ scissors
- ▣ ruler
- ▣ pencil
- ▣ craft knife
- ▣ $3\frac{1}{2}$- by $7\frac{1}{4}$-inch piece of posterboard
- ▣ craft glue
- ▣ tape
- ▣ green and red plastic adhesive covering
- ▣ various craft materials (wiggle eyes, yarn, rickrack, felt, ribbon, glitter, and so on)
- ▣ fine-point permanent marker
- ▣ 3- by 5-inch cards, cut in half

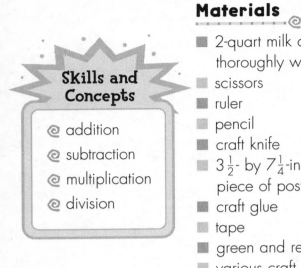

Making the Monster Math-Muncher Machine

1. Open the top of the carton and cut apart the flaps. Turn the carton over and use the bottom as the top for the math-muncher machine.

2. Using the ruler and pencil, draw a line 2 inches from the top across one side of the carton. Draw another line $2\frac{1}{2}$ inches from the top. Then, on the same side, draw two more lines the same distances from the bottom. Cut along each line, then cut out the $\frac{1}{2}$-inch strip of carton between each set of lines. When finished, you will have two $\frac{1}{2}$-inch slits spaced approximately $2\frac{1}{2}$ inches apart.

3. To make a ramp inside the carton, turn the carton over and squeeze a line of glue into the top corner of the slitted side. Firmly push one end of the posterboard piece into the glue. Allow the glue to dry.

4. Turn the carton upright. Slide the loose end of the posterboard through the bottom slit and fold it a $\frac{1}{2}$-inch over the edge. Tape the end in place.

5. Close and tape the carton flaps in place.

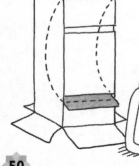

6 Cover the section between the slits with red plastic covering (this is the monster's mouth). Cover the rest of the carton with green covering.

7 To decorate, glue on wiggle eyes, yarn hair, and rickrack or construction paper teeth. (So that the drill cards slide through the machine smoothly, make sure the teeth do not extend over the edge of the bottom slit.) Add other features as desired.

8 For each drill card, use the permanent marker to write a problem at the top of the tall end of the card. Flip the card over from bottom to top and write the answer at the bottom of the back side of the card. Prepare a grade-level set of cards for basic facts in addition, subtraction, multiplication, and division.

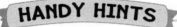

HANDY HINTS

▲ "Pop" bubbles in the plastic adhesive covering by poking them with a straight pin and pressing the air out.

▲ Additional cards can be created to provide practice in comparing numbers, matching numerals to number words, telling time, identifying fractions and coins, and other math skills.

Ways to Use the Monster Math-Muncher Machine

◆ Give a child a set of fact cards related to the skill you want to reinforce. Have the child select a card, read the problem, and give the answer. Then ask the child to insert the top end of the card into the top slit of the machine. When the card slides out of the bottom slit, it will land answer-up.

◆ Give children a supply of "monster food" counters (plastic bugs or dried beans). Invite them to use the counters to solve each problem fed to the machine.

◆ Invite student pairs to use the machine and bean counters in a game. Partners take turns answering problems on the cards and running them through the muncher to check answers. For each correct answer, a player takes a bean. After all the cards have been processed, players count their beans. The player with the most beans wins the game.

◆ For group work, one child operates the machine. He or she shows a problem to the group members, who write their answers on paper (or the mini math boards from page 44). Then the operator runs the card through the muncher and holds up the correct answer for children to check their answers.

Pizza Multiplication Wheels

Flavor your multiplication and division drill with a student favorite—pizza!

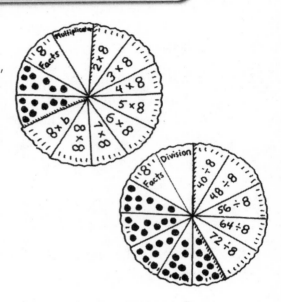

Skills and Concepts

@ multiplication facts

@ division facts

Materials

- ◼ divided circle pattern, page 56
- ◼ 18 10-inch sturdy yellow paper plates
- ◼ pencil with dull point
- ◼ ruler
- ◼ black fine-point permanent marker
- ◼ scissors
- ◼ 405 red sticker dots
- ◼ dried beans

Making the Pizza Multiplication Wheels

1 To divide each plate into 12 sections, center the circle pattern on the plate. Use the pencil and ruler to trace each line on the circle, pressing firmly so that an impression is left on the plate surface. After all the lines have been traced, remove the pattern. Then, using the line impressions as guides, use a permanent marker and ruler to draw each line directly on the plate. Be sure to extend each line to the edge of the plate.

2 Cut along one line to the center of each plate. Then separate the plates into nine pairs.

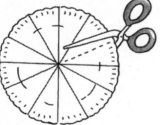

3 To label the plate pairs, position each plate with the cut section at 12 o'clock. On one plate, use the permanent marker to write "Multiplication" on the first section to the right of the cut and a fact-family name, such as "8 Facts," on the second section (this will be the equation plate). On the other plate (the pizza plate), write "Multiplication" on the first section to the left of the cut and the fact-family name on the second section. Be sure to label a pair of plates for each fact family from 1 to 9.

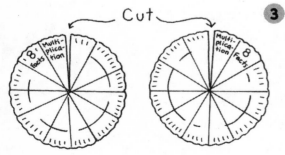

Cut

4 For each equation plate, write an equation for the fact family on each section to the right of the label. For example, for the "8 Facts," the first equation will be "0 x 8," the second "1 x 8," then "2 x 8," and so on, up to "9 x 8."

5 To prepare each pizza plate, count out 10 sets of sticker dots ("pepperoni") for the fact family labeled on the plate. For instance, you will need 10 sets of 8 dots for the "8 Facts." Affix one set of dots on each section to the left of the labeled section.

6 To assemble each multiplication wheel, place the equation plate over the pizza plate, aligning the two plates at the cut. Be sure to position the cut at 12 o'clock.

7 Bend the plates to the right of the cut slightly away from you. Then turn the equation plate counterclockwise (left) so that the "Multiplication" section moves behind the "Multiplication" section of the pizza plate. Continue to turn the equation plate until the cut edge of the pizza plate lines up next to the first section with an equation. On the example, this will be "0 x 8."

8 Turn the multiplication wheel over. Use the permanent marker to write "Answer" along the exposed cut edge of the pizza plate. Then write the answer to the equation ("0") directly below the cut edge. The answer will actually be written on the back of the equation plate.

9 Working from the front of the multiplication wheel to the back, continue turning the equation plate until you reach each section with an equation (the next one will be "1 x 8"). Then flip the wheel and record the answer on the back, as in step 8.

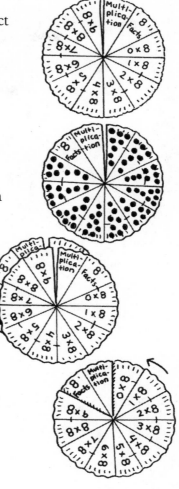

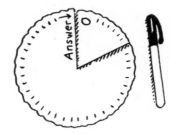

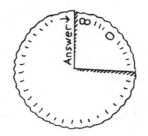

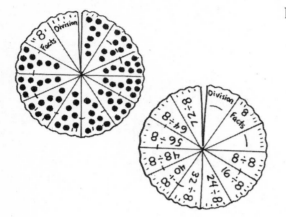

Variation

With a few simple modifications, you can convert this project into a division wheel!

1. Follow the directions to step 7, labeling the plates with "Division" and division sentences for the fact family, as shown. Note that the first section to the right of the fact-family label is left blank for the division wheel.

2. In steps 8 and 9, write the answer for each division equation on the back of the wheel.

HANDY HINTS

▲ If preferrred, you can use a protractor to draw the sections on the plates. To do this, locate the center of each plate. Then measure and mark every 30-degree angle with a protractor and pencil. Finally, use a ruler and pencil to draw the lines for the sections.

▲ To help children visually track their place on the wheel, use a red marker to edge the cut side of the blank section on the pizza wheel.

Ways to Use the Pizza Wheels

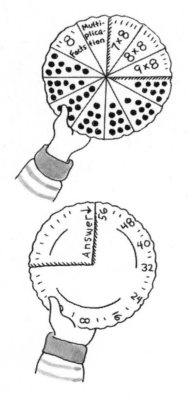

◆ Have children use the multiplication and division wheels to practice basic facts. To use, a child turns the equation plate until the cut edge of the pizza plate lines up with the section for the desired equation. For multiplication, the child counts the exposed dots to find the answer to the equation. He or she counts the number of exposed sections (or slices) to find the answer for division. To check each answer, the child turns the wheel over and looks at the number just below the answer label.

◆ Give children a supply of beans and the multiplication or division wheel. Ask them to set the wheel to an equation and determine the answer. Then have children count out a quantity of beans equal to their answer. (For division, they will group the beans in sets.) To check their bean count, instruct them to place one bean on each exposed pepperoni on the wheel. Afterward, have children remove the beans and check the back of the wheel for the answer.

◆ Ask children to answer word problems with the wheels. For example, you might ask them to tell you how many pepperonis are on three slices of pizza. Students will use the multiplication wheel to figure and check their answers (on the example, the answer is "24"). Or you might have them tell how many slices of pizza will hold 24 pepperonis. Using the division wheel, children find and check their answers ("3").

◆ Invite student pairs to use a wheel and a supply of sticky notes in two different colors to use as flags in this game. To begin, each child chooses a flag color. Then the pair agrees on a multiplication or division wheel to use. The first child calls out which slice of pizza he or she wants on the wheel, identifying it by the equation. Then he or she names the answer to the problem, sets the wheel on the problem, and checks the back for the answer. If correct, the child marks that slice of pizza with his or her flag color. If incorrect, it remains unmarked. The second child repeats the process, calling out any unflagged pizza slices on the wheel. Students continue in this manner until all slices have been flagged. The child with the most flagged slices wins that round.

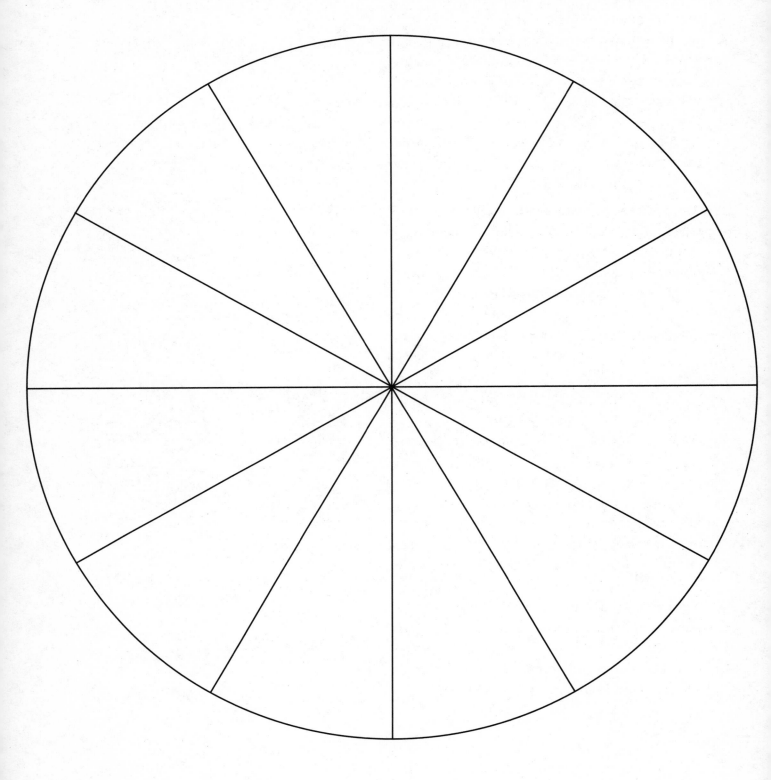

Nifty Nonstandard Rulers

These easy-to-make rulers really measure up with students.

Materials

- 1½-inch-wide strips of white or light colored posterboard
- various objects suitable for nonstandard measure (paper clips, toothpicks, dried pinto beans, and so on)
- craft glue
- scissors
- black fine-point permanent marker

Skills and Concepts

- nonstandard units of measure
- place value

Making the Nifty Nonstandard Rulers

1 To make a ruler, select a set of 10 objects, such as paper clips. Glue the objects end to end onto a strip of posterboard. Cut off the excess posterboard.

2 Repeat step 1 to make several rulers with the same type of objects.

3 Use the permanent marker to mark and label a few of each ruler type with numerals, starting with the item on the left and moving to the right.

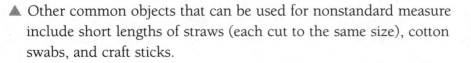

HANDY HINTS

▲ Other common objects that can be used for nonstandard measure include short lengths of straws (each cut to the same size), cotton swabs, and craft sticks.

▲ You may also want to construct a marked ruler with 100 bean "units." You can use this ruler as an example of how the numbered units on a ruler make measurement tasks more simple.

▲ Remind children to express their measurements in the proper units. For example, a sheet of paper might measure 9 paper clips wide. Or it might be 4 toothpicks wide. Emphasize the importance of including both the number and the units used for measuring.

Ways to Use the Nifty Nonstandard Rulers

◆ Introduce children to measurement by having them measure classroom objects with sets of the loose objects you used for the nonstandard rulers. As they work, guide children to understand that using a row of loose objects is the most efficient way to measure an object. Then present the unmarked rulers to students. Have them measure objects shorter than the rulers and compare the experience to measuring with loose objects. Children will discover that measuring with a ruler is much easier!

◆ Have pairs of children find objects longer than the unmarked rulers. Give them more than one unmarked ruler to measure the objects. After measuring with several rulers, take all but one from the partners. Then have students measure longer objects with just one ruler. (You may need to demonstrate how to mark the ruler's length several times against the object in order to measure it completely.) To figure the object's measurement, children count each ruler length as 10 units and then include any additional individual units in their answers.

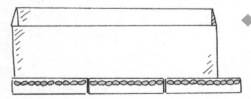

◆ After children successfully measure objects with unmarked rulers, invite them to use the marked rulers. As they measure, instruct children to read the numerals on the ruler rather than count the units. Explain that standard rulers are marked similarly, so counting the units is not necessary. This activity will provide a bridge for students to measure with standard units. (To make the transition less confusing, make sure the standard rulers are marked with only inch or centimeter units, instead of both.)

2 tens
7 ones

◆ Use the marked nonstandard rulers to reinforce the concept of place value. First, have students write their measurement findings in tens and ones. To do this, they simply count the number of ruler lengths to determine the tens value. Then they count the number of any additional individual units to find the ones value. Finally, ask children to write the measurement as a whole number.

Checkered Measurement Boards

These checkered boards are perfectly designed to help students understand the concepts of perimeter and area.

Materials

- checkered fabric with squares of 1 inch and 1 centimeter
- scissors
- heavy posterboard
- fabric glue
- black permanent marker
- grid patterns, pages 61–62
- clear overhead transparencies
- wipe-off pen
- paper towels

Making the Checkered Measurement Boards

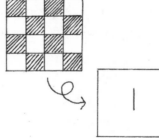

1. Cut out different-size rectangles from each type of fabric, always cutting along the checkered pattern.

2. Glue each piece of fabric to the posterboard. After the glue has dried, cut out each fabric board. Use the permanent marker to label the back of each board with a different number.

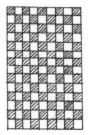

3. To make transparent grid overlays for student use, photocopy both grid patterns onto separate transparencies. (You may wish to make several overlays for each grid.)

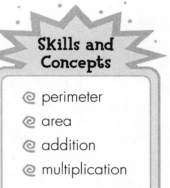

4. To use an overlay and measurement board together, a child places the grid over the board, aligning the top left corner with the checks on the fabric. The child then uses a wipe-off pen to number the squares to figure either the perimeter or area of the board. When finished, the child erases the numbers on the overlay, using a paper towel.

5. Ask children to record their findings in the appropriate units— inches, centimeters, square inches, or square centimeters.

Skills and Concepts

- perimeter
- area
- addition
- multiplication

HANDY HINTS

▲ If fabric with 1-inch or 1-centimeter squares is not available, use any other square pattern that is available. Do not use the provided grid patterns with these boards. Also be sure to have students record their measurements for perimeter and area in units or square units (instead of inches or centimeters).

▲ If you don't have access to a copy machine that photocopies transparencies, trace the grid patterns onto transparencies with a permanent marker.

Ways to Use the Checkered Measurement Boards

Board 1
Length = 5 inches
Width = 4 inches

◆ To find perimeter in this activity, children can elect to use the grid overlay if desired. First, ask children to write the number for each board on a sheet of paper. Have them count the number of squares in the length and width of each board and then write these measurements beside the corresponding number. (Remind children to use the appropriate units.) After students measure the boards, have them compare their results.

◆ To find the perimeter of each board, have children count the squares along each edge. Then ask them to add the numbers together and report their findings in the appropriate units. If desired, students can use the appropriate grid overlay as a counting aid.

◆ Ask students to count the total number of squares on a board to find its area (they can use the appropriate grid overlay, if desired). Use this activity as a springboard for teaching children how to compute area with multiplication and to introduce the formula for finding area: A = L x W.

◆ Invite children to create their own boards from the leftover pieces of checkered fabric (or they can use checkered wrapping paper). Have them figure the perimeter and area for each of their boards and write these on the back. To use, children exchange boards with classmates. Then they measure for perimeter and area and write their findings on sticky notes. Finally, they turn the boards over to check their answers.

◆ Use a wipe-off pen to outline shapes on the grid overlays. Have children place the overlays over fabric with corresponding-size checks and then figure the perimeter or area for the shapes.

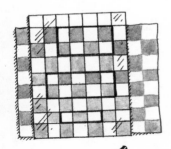

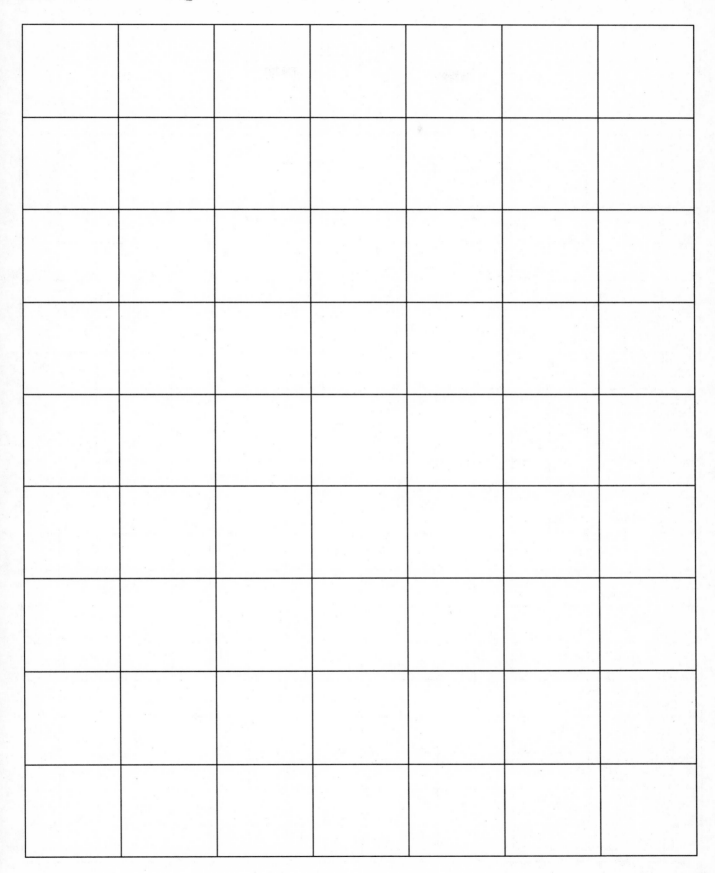

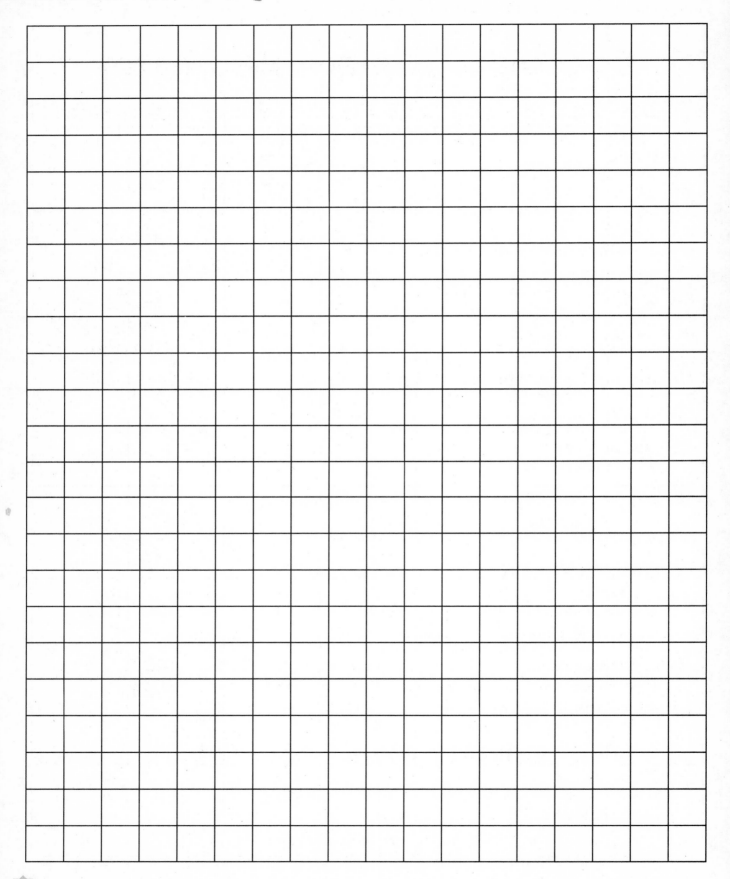

Chocolate Square Geometry

Add some flavor to computing the perimeter and area of geometric shapes with this sweet activity.

Materials

- 1-inch square ceramic tiles (available at home-improvement and craft stores)
- newspaper
- dark brown nontoxic spray enamel
- magnetic tape
- chocolate squares pattern, page 65
- one-inch grid pattern, page 61
- steel cookie sheet

Skills and Concepts

- perimeter
- area
- addition
- multiplication

Making the Chocolate Square Manipulatives

1. Remove the webbing from the back of each ceramic tile.

2. Outdoors, or in a well-ventilated area, spread the tiles right side up on newspaper.

3. Spray-paint the tiles so that the tops and sides are completely covered with brown paint. If necessary, apply several coats of paint, allowing the paint to dry between coatings.

4. When the "chocolate" tiles are thoroughly dry and no longer tacky to the touch, attach a strip of magnetic tape to the back of each one. Make sure the magnet supports the weight of the tile when it is attached to a vertical surface.

5. Set the tiles aside on a hard, flat surface. Then place a heavy weight on top of them for at least a week. This will flatten the magnetic tape so that it adheres more securely to the tile.

HANDY HINTS

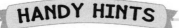

▲ You may wish to paint the tiles with a primer before applying the brown enamel.

▲ If you are unable to find 1-inch tiles, you can use 1-inch wood squares instead (available at craft stores).

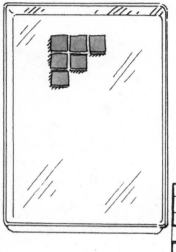

▲ If possible, provide children with chocolate bars divided into small squares to use as an additional manipulative. To use, have them create a candy bar shape with the chocolate tiles and reproduce it with their real chocolate squares. After the activity, invite children to take their chocolates home for an after-school snack. (Be sure to check for food allergies first!)

▲ Store the chocolate squares in a "chocolates" box or tin.

Ways to Use the Chocolate Square Manipulatives

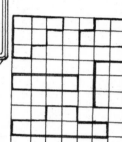

◆ Invite students to use the chocolate squares to create geometric patterns on the cookie sheet. Then, after working with the squares and various shapes, give children copies of the chocolate squares pattern. Ask them to duplicate the patterns using the chocolates and cookie sheet. If a child has difficulty with this activity, instruct him or her to cut out each shape, place it on the cookie sheet, and then cover it with chocolate squares.

◆ Alternatively, have children create shapes with the chocolate squares. Then ask them to fill in their chocolate square shapes on copies of the grid pattern. When finished, students can exchange grids and use the chocolate squares to reproduce their classmates' shapes.

◆ Give children specific dimensions for the length and width of a chocolate bar. Have them create the chocolate bar on the cookie sheet. Then have them figure its perimeter and area. Afterward, invite children to "eat" parts of the chocolate bar. After each "bite," challenge students to again figure its perimeter and area. (Make sure students don't really bite the ceramic chocolates since they could break their teeth on them!)

◆ Arrange the chocolate squares into rectangles and squares of different sizes. Ask children to figure the length and width of each shape. Then have them use addition to determine the perimeter of each shape, or multiply to find the area.

◆ Tell students to assemble a candy bar with several chocolate squares. Then have them measure, cut out, and design a wrapper for the bar. After they've wrapped the "candy," have students each ask a classmate to estimate its area and perimeter.

Sugar-Cube Volume Boxes

Sugar-coat the concept of volume with these special sugar cubes and boxes.

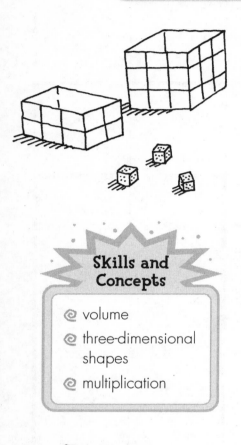

Skills and Concepts

- @ volume
- @ three-dimensional shapes
- @ multiplication

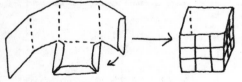

Materials

- ■ $\frac{3}{8}$-inch wood cubes (available at craft stores)
- ▨ white glue-paint (a mixture of two parts craft glue and one part paint)
- ■ white glitter
- ▨ waxed paper
- ■ heavyweight white paper
- ▨ sugar-cube volume box patterns, pages 68–69
- ■ pencil
- ▨ laminator
- ■ scissors
- ▨ craft glue

Making the Sugar-Cube Volume Boxes

1. To make sugar cubes, coat each wood cube with glue-paint and then cover it with glitter. Set the cubes on waxed paper to dry.

2. Copy each sugar-cube box pattern onto heavyweight white paper.

3. Laminate the patterns and cut them out.

4. To assemble each box, fold and glue the pattern as shown.

⟩ HANDY HINTS ⟨

▲ If desired, you can use tape on the outside of the box to help hold the box tabs in place while the glue dries.

▲ Fill a variety of small jewelry boxes with sugar cubes to see if the volume can be measured accurately. If the cubes fit snugly in a box, and are level with the top of the box, then add this box to your collection of sugar-cube boxes for classroom use.

▲ For variety, you may wish to use real sugar cubes for the activities. (Note: These may not be as durable as the wood cubes.)

Ways to Use the Sugar-Cube Volume Boxes

◆ Invite children to fill the boxes with the sugar cubes. Then have them empty the contents and count the number of cubes that were in each box. Explain that this number represents the volume of each box in sugar-cube units. (Because the sugar cubes are so close in size to a cubic centimeter, you might ask students to report the volume in cubic centimeters, or cm^3.)

◆ Present children with several boxes and ask them to predict which box has the most volume. Then have them fill each box, empty and count the cubes, and compare their results.

◆ Have children work in pairs. Have one child build an irregular three-dimensional shape, such as stairs. Ask the child's partner to duplicate the shape. Then ask both children to compare and count the sugar cubes in their shapes to determine whether or not they are identical.

◆ Give each child a box and sugar cubes. Have children use the sugar cubes to build a box shape to match the dimensions of the real box. When children complete the sugar-cube box, have them transfer it into the actual box to see if it is a perfect fit.

◆ Use the sugar cubes and boxes to introduce advanced students to the formula for volume. First, have children use sugar cubes to build a box to match the dimensions of a real box. Then explain that their sugar-cube box is made of layers. Have students carefully remove the top layer of their box and place it on the table. Show them how to calculate the area of the layer by multiplying its length and width (L x W). Then tell students that each layer in their box has the same area as the top layer. (You might have them prove this by removing each layer and computing its area.) Next, ask childen to return the top layer to the box and then count the number of layers in the box. Explain that this number equals the height of their box. To find the volume of the box, have children multiply the area of one layer by the height of the box. Then ask them to count the cubes in their box and compare the results to see if the two numbers are the same. Finally, show children the formula for volume (V = L x W x H), and have them use it to find the volume for other boxes.

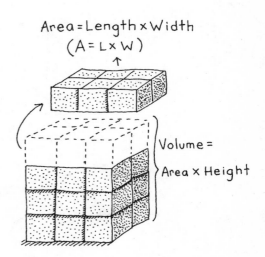

Area = Length × Width
(A = L × W)

Volume = Area × Height

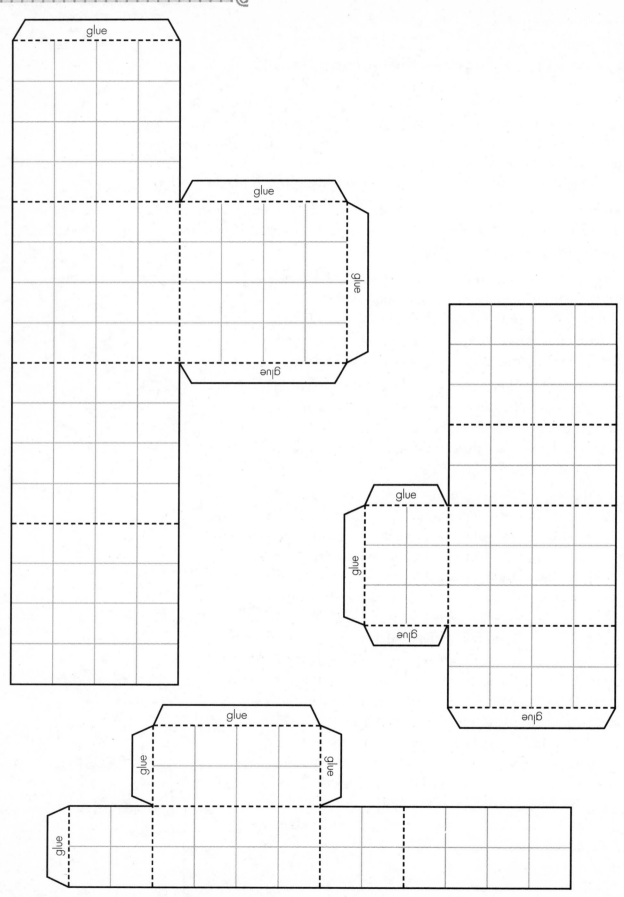

Sugar-Cube Volume Box Patterns

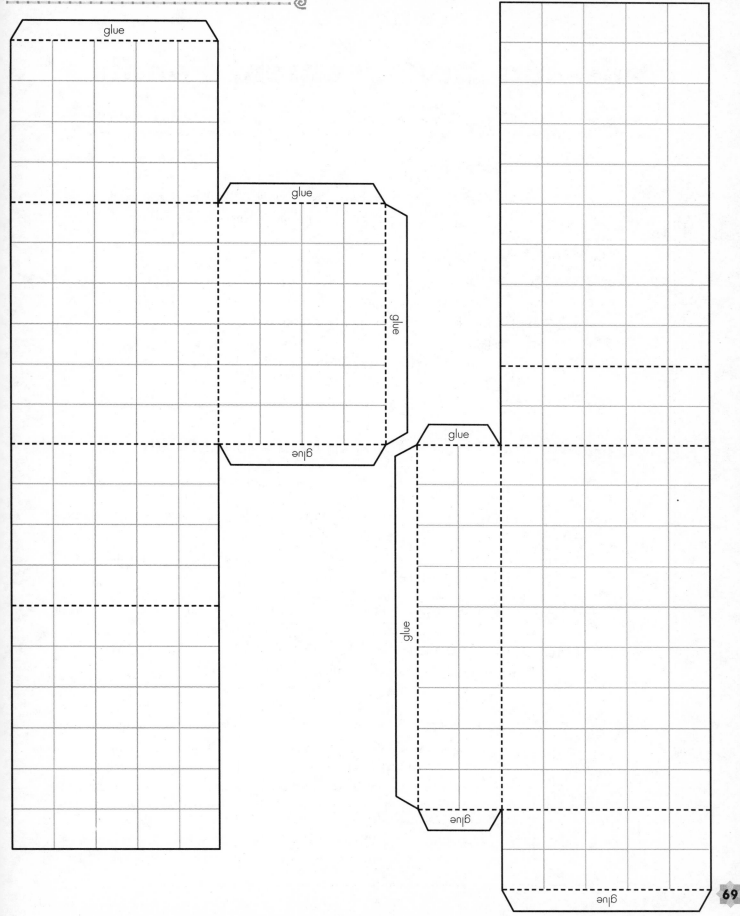

Milk-Jug Measurement Family

C'mon and join this milk-jug family for a fun-filled gathering of liquid measurement skills!

Skills and Concepts

- liquid units of measure
- relationships
- addition
- subtraction

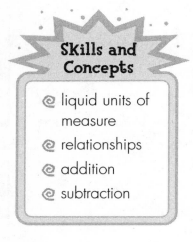

Materials

- clear plastic container in each of the following sizes: gallon, half-gallon, quart, pint, and half-pint (milk jugs and juice bottles work well)
- 1-cup measuring cup
- water
- plastic funnel
- black fine-point permanent marker

OPTIONAL

- various craft materials (including wiggle eyes, craft foam, and paint pens)
- water-resistant craft glue (follow directions on package)

Making the Milk-Jug Measurement Family

1. Thoroughly clean and dry each container and remove labels.

2. Fill the measuring cup to the 1-cup line. Pour the water through the funnel into the half-pint container. Use the permanent marker to mark a line at the waterline on the container. Pour the water out and label the mark "1 cup."

3. For the pint container, add one cup of water and mark the waterline. Then add another cup of water and mark the new waterline. Pour out the water and label each mark to show the corresponding number of cups, as well as the half-pint level (which will be even with the 1-cup mark).

4. Repeat step 3 for each of the remaining containers, adding and marking one cup of water at a time until the container is full. After you discard the water, be sure to label each container with the corresponding number of cups and the measure for each smaller container.

5. OPTIONAL: If desired, use the craft materials to decorate each container to resemble a face. (Decorate the surface opposite the marked measurements.)

HANDY HINTS

▲ Select water-resistant craft materials to decorate the containers, since children will be using liquid in and around the containers.

▲ In addition to liquids, provide uncooked popcorn, rice, beans, and other similar substances for children to use in their measuring activities.

▲ Have children use the funnel to pour water and other materials into the containers.

▲ You may wish to make measuring containers of different shapes and then use these to demonstrate the concept of conservation. To extend, invite students to collect and make personal sets of containers to use at home.

Ways to Use the Milk-Jug Measurement Family

◆ Instruct children to line up the containers in random order on a table. Then have them add one cup of water to each container and compare the waterlines. After children have shared their observations, ask them to add another cup of water to each container and compare. Have children continue adding water, one cup at a time, until every container is full. Each time a container is filled, ask children to move it to another part of the table, keeping the containers in order. When finished, the container "family" will be sequenced by volume.

◆ Invite students to measure cups of water (or dry substances, such as uncooked rice) into the smaller containers. Then have them transfer the contents to larger containers and describe the relationships between those members of the measurement family.

◆ Conversely, have children pour amounts from the large containers into the small containers. To do this, they fill the 1-cup measuring cup and then transfer the water to a small container. Encourage children to describe the relationship between the containers each time a transfer is made.

◆ Have children create and solve addition and subtraction problems with the family of measurement containers. For example, they can write an equation for adding the cups in one quart and one pint (4 cups + 2 cups) and then find the sum (6 cups). Or they might compute how many more cups are in a gallon than in a half-gallon (16 cups – 8 cups = 8 cups).

Liquid Liter Lizard

Children will leap into learning about the metric system with this liter-loving lizard.

Skills and Concepts

- liquid units of measure
- relationships
- estimation
- addition

Materials

- transparent green, plastic 2-liter soft drink bottle
- 100 mL graduated cylinder with milliliter increments (you might borrow this from a science class)
- plastic funnel
- water
- black fine-point permanent marker
- several smaller clear, plastic containers in various shapes (tall, short, and stout)

OPTIONAL
- liter lizard patterns, page 74
- sheet of green craft foam
- pencil
- scissors
- water-resistant craft glue (follow directions on package)
- large wiggle eyes
- small piece of red craft foam

Making the Liquid Liter Lizard

1. Thoroughly clean and dry all containers and remove labels.

2. Fill the graduated cylinder to the 100 mL line. Pour the water through the funnel into the 2-liter bottle. Then use the permanent marker to mark a line at the waterline on the bottle. Label the mark "100 mL."

3. Repeat step 2, adding another 100 mL of water and marking the bottle "200 mL" at the new line. Continue in this manner, marking and labeling each 100 mL increment until you reach "2,000 mL."

4. For each smaller bottle, add and mark as many 100 mL increments of water as possible, without overfilling the bottle.

5. Use a permanent marker to draw a lizard on the 2-liter bottle.

6. OPTIONAL: Using the lizard pattern, trace the outline of the lizard head and tail once and the arms and legs twice onto the green craft foam. Cut out the shapes, then fill in details with the permanent marker. Add wiggle eyes and a red craft-foam tongue. Glue each piece to the bottle to create a lizard, as shown.

HANDY HINTS

▲ In addition to liquids, provide uncooked popcorn, rice, beans, and other similar substances for children to use in their measuring activities.

▲ If you're unable to locate a graduated cylinder, use a measuring cup marked with mL increments.

▲ You might provide plastic measuring containers for student use.

▲ Have children use the funnel to pour water and other substances into the containers.

Ways to Use the Liquid Liter Lizard

◆ Instruct children to line up the liter lizard and other containers in random order on a table. Have them add 100 mL of water to each container and compare the waterlines. Then ask them to add another 100 mL of water to each container and compare. Have children continue adding water in 100 mL increments until every container is filled to the top line. Ask children to move each filled container to another part of the table, sequencing them in the order in which they are filled. When finished, have children observe the sequence. Are they surprised at the results?

◆ Invite students to measure water (or dry substances, such as uncooked rice) in 100 mL increments into the smaller containers. Then have them transfer the contents to the liter lizard. Ask children to describe the relationships between smaller containers and the lizard bottle.

◆ Have children estimate how many times the liquid from the lizard will fill a selected smaller bottle. To test their estimates, students pour water from the lizard into the graduated cylinder in increments of 100 mL. They transfer the water into the small bottle until it is full, record a mark on paper for each full bottle and then pour the water into a pitcher for future use. Students continue filling and emptying the small bottle until the lizard is empty. Then they count their marks to discover how many times the small bottle was completely filled. Have children compare their results with their estimates.

◆ Have children create and solve addition problems with the liter lizard and smaller containers. For example, they can add the liquid amounts in two different containers (such as 200 mL + 400 mL), figure the answer, and then pour the water from the two containers into the liter lizard to check their answer.

Giant Magnetic Clock

Tick-tock, giant clock! This easy-to-assemble clock will be a big hit with students.

Materials

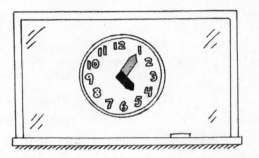

- 2- by 10-inch strip of sturdy black posterboard
- 2- by 15-inch strip of sturdy red posterboard
- scissors
- laminator
- magnetic tape
- large magnetic chalkboard
- chalkboard compass
- chalk

Making the Giant Magnetic Clock

1. To make clock hands, cut one end of the black and red posterboard strips into an arrow. The black arrow will be used for the hour hand and the red arrow will be the minute hand. Laminate each piece.

2. Attach several strips of magnetic tape to one side of each clock hand. Make sure the magnets will support the weight of the hand when it is placed on the magnetic chalkboard.

3. Use the compass and chalk to draw a 3-foot circle on the chalkboard.

4. Write the numerals 1 to 12 inside the circle to create a giant clock.

5. Attach the hour and minute hands to the giant clock.

Skills and Concepts

- number recognition
- telling time
- skip-counting
- problem-solving

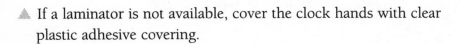

HANDY HINTS

⚠ If a laminator is not available, cover the clock hands with clear plastic adhesive covering.

▲ To draw a circle without a chalkboard compass, tie a length of string around a chalk stick, leaving a loose end 18 inches long. Hold the end of the string firmly against the center of the board, then draw a circle around the center point, keeping the string taut as you draw.

Ways to Use the Giant Magnetic Clock

◆ Introduce children to the giant clock by placing only one clock hand at a time on the chalkboard clock and explaining how it is used in time-telling. Then, using both clock hands, have children practice telling time to the hour. Also invite children to take turns setting the giant clock to the hour.

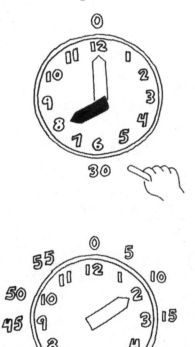

◆ Give children practice in telling time to the half- and quarter-hour. First, write "0" on the outside of the clock at the number 12. Explain that this indicates time to the hour. Then write "30" (for the half-hour) outside the clock at the 6. Next, set the clock to different hour and half-hour designations, each time asking students to name the time. Later, write "15" and "45" outside the clock at the numbers 3 and 9, respectively. Then set the clock to the half- or quarter-hour and have children tell the time.

◆ Around the outer edge of the giant clock, write the five-minute increment corresponding to each clock numeral. Remove the hour hand. Then point the minute hand to different numbers. Ask children to name the five-minute increment for each number to which the hand points. Later, add the hour hand and have children practice telling time to five minutes.

◆ Present children with a variety of problems to solve with the giant clock. For example, you might set the clock to 7:00, then ask students to tell how many hours have passed since 4:00. To provide practice in writing time designations, have children record their responses on paper (or on the mini math boards from page 44).

Magnificent Magnetic Clocks

These clocks are the main attraction when it comes to learning time concepts.

Materials

- 10-inch round, iron or steel stove-burner cover per child (light, solid colors work best)
- black fine-point permanent marker
- $\frac{1}{2}$- by 3-inch strip of sturdy black posterboard
- $\frac{1}{2}$- by 4-inch strip of sturdy red posterboard
- laminator
- magnetic tape

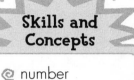

Skills and Concepts

- number recognition
- telling time
- skip-counting
- problem-solving

Making the Magnificent Magnetic Clocks

1. Use the permanent marker to write the 12 clock numbers on the top surface of each stove-burner cover.

2. Mark the center of each stove-burner cover with a black dot.

3. To make clock hands, cut one end of the black and red posterboard strips into an arrow. The black arrow will be used for the hour hand and the red arrow will be the minute hand. Laminate each piece.

4. Attach a piece of magnetic tape to the straight end of each clock arrow.

5. Attach the hour and minute hands to each clock.

HANDY HINTS

▲ To make the clock numbers more uniform, you may wish to use a number stencil to draw them on the clocks.

▲ If a laminator is not available, cover the clock hands with clear plastic adhesive covering.

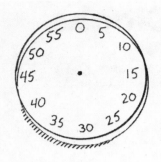

▲ You may wish to make a "minute" clock on the other side of each stove-burner cover. Simply write the five-minute increment corresponding to each clock number, rather than the number itself, on the inside of the stove-burner cover. Then mark a dot at the center of the clock. Instruct children to use only the red minute hand on their minute clocks.

▲ If desired, use these individual magnetic clocks along with the giant magnetic clock on page 75.

Ways to Use the Magnificent Magnetic Clocks

◆ Have children use only the black hour hand to set their clocks to a specific hour. Once children understand that the short, black hand indicates the hour, have them place the longer, red minute hand on their clocks and point it to 12. Explain that with the minute hand in this position, the time is set to the exact hour. Then have students again point their hour hands to different numbers and name the time to the hour.

◆ Give children practice in telling time to the half- and quarter-hour. First, use a wipe-off pen to write a small "0" on the clock just under the number 12. Explain that this indicates time to the hour. Then write "30" (for the half-hour) above the 6. Have children set their clocks to the hour and half-hour by pointing their minute hands to either the 12 or 6. Later add "15" and "45" next to the numbers 3 and 9, respectively. Then have children set their clocks to name times to the half- or quarter-hour. When finished with this skill, erase the additional numbers with a paper towel.

◆ To teach telling time to five minutes, have children turn their clocks over. Then call out five-minute increments of time. Have children point their minute hands to the corresponding number. To help children associate the five-minute increments with the actual clock numbers, use a wipe-off pen to write the corresponding five-minute increment next to each number on the front of their magnetic clocks. Attach both the hour and minute hands. Then have children practice telling time to five minutes. When finished with this skill, erase the additional numbers with a paper towel.

◆ Present children with a variety of problems to solve with their individual magnetic clocks. To provide practice in writing time designations, have children write their responses on paper. When children become more skilled at telling time, student partners can work together to make up and solve problems with their clocks.

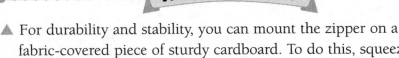

Digital Zipper Clock

This special clock provides a zippy way for children to learn how to tell time with a digital clock.

Materials

- 26-inch light colored zipper (coat zippers work well)
- black and red ultra-fine-point permanent markers
- ruler

Making the Digital Zipper Clock

1. Working from the bottom to the top of the zipper (not the zipper tape), measure and mark 24 one-inch intervals on the right zipper tape along the length of the zipper.

2. Use the red marker to label the first mark at the bottom of the zipper "12:00." Then label the second mark "1:00," the third "2:00," and so on, labeling each mark with an hour increment up to 11:00.

3. Use the black marker to label the next mark "12:00." Then, as in step 2, continue labeling the marks with hour increments up to "11:00."

4. Label the last mark with a red "12:00."

5. On the left zipper tape, write a red "A.M." next to each red 12:00 (at the bottom and top of the zipper). Write a black "P.M." next to the black 12:00 (in the middle).

Skills and Concepts

- telling time
- A.M. and P.M.
- elapsed and future time
- problem-solving

HANDY HINTS

▲ For durability and stability, you can mount the zipper on a fabric-covered piece of sturdy cardboard. To do this, squeeze a thin line of fabric glue along the edges of the zipper tape. Wipe away any excess glue, making sure it does not ooze onto the zipper teeth. Then carefully press the zipped zipper onto the fabric board. Allow the glue to dry thoroughly before using the zipper.

Ways to Use the Digital Zipper Clock

◆ To teach how time progresses from A.M. to P.M., have children open the zipper completely. Explain that the time shown, 12:00 A.M., represents midnight and the beginning of a new day. Then have students move the zipper from hour to hour until it reaches 12:00 P.M., in the middle of the zipper. Tell them that this time represents noon, or the middle of the day (the placement of this time in the middle of the zipper serves as a nice visual reminder of this concept). Ask children to continue zipping the zipper until it reaches 12:00 A.M. at the top. Explain that one day has now ended and a new day will begin. Then have children open the zipper completely to begin the new day.

◆ Use the zipper clock to reinforce the progression of time and how it relates to the days of the week. To do this, have children open the zipper completely. Tell them that this time represents the beginning of a new day—Monday. Then have students slowly zip the zipper, describing Monday activities that occur on or about every corresponding hour on the zipper (they can refer to their class and personal schedules). When the zipper reaches the top, explain that Monday has ended and it's time for Tuesday to begin. Then have children open the zipper completely once again and zip through Tuesday's schedule. Repeat for each day of the week.

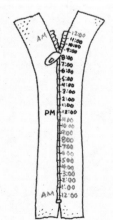

◆ Invite children to use the zipper clock to practice telling time on a digital clock. To begin, call out a time to the hour, including A.M. or P.M., and have children set the zipper clock to the given time. After some practice, set a digital clock to a specific hour, then have children name the time and set the zipper clock to match. Later, student partners can take turns operating the real and zipper digital clocks.

◆ Set up elapsed- and future-time problems for children to solve. An example might be "If a child ate breakfast at 8:00 A.M. and it is now 1:00 P.M., how much time has passed since breakfast?" Or "If it's 2:00 P.M. now, how long is the wait for a 7:00 P.M. baseball game to start?" To solve the problems, children set the zipper clock to the "current" time and then zip it forward or backward to find the answers. Additionally, the zipper clock can be used to solve reasoning problems, such as "What time do I need to arrive at the airport if my plane leaves at 11:00 A.M. and I must check in two hours before takeoff?"

Giant Magnetic Money

> Children will cash in on some huge learning with this giant set of money.

Materials

- giant money patterns, pages 83–85
- crayons
- posterboard
- glue
- laminator
- magnetic tape
- magnetic chalkboard or display board

Making the Giant Magnetic Money

1 Copy the money patterns as many times as desired.

2 Color each bill and coin to resemble real money.

3 Glue each piece of money onto posterboard. Cut out the money and then laminate it for durability.

4 Back each piece of money with magnetic tape.

Skills and Concepts

- money recognition
- money values
- skip-counting
- problem-solving

HANDY HINTS

▲ If desired, enlarge the money patterns even more, making sure you enlarge each pattern proportionately.

▲ If possible, copy the patterns onto appropriately colored paper. This will eliminate the need to color the money and will also give it a more uniform look.

▲ Cover the money with clear plastic adhesive covering if a laminator is not available.

Ways to Use the Giant Magnetic Money

◆ Introduce children to each bill and coin by displaying its front and back on the board. Review the value of each. Then place different amounts of the given bill or coin on the board. Work with children to help them figure the value of the money displayed. You may wish to use the nickels, dimes, quarters, and 5-, 10-, and 20-dollar bills to reinforce skip-counting with students.

◆ Arrange the money to represent different amounts. Use bills, a combination of coins, or a combination of both bills and coins. Invite children to tell the value of the money shown. Alternatively, have children take turns displaying sets of money on the board for the class to count. Ask the child responsible for the money set to write its value on a sticky note. Then, after students have shared their answers, have the child show them the correct answer.

◆ Use the giant money to help children understand the relationship between the different coins and bills. For example, you might put five nickels on the board and ask children to tell their value. When they respond, replace the nickels with a quarter, explaining that five nickels and one quarter have the same value. Similarly, you might demonstrate how four quarters equals the value of a dollar, or four 5-dollar bills equals the value of a 20-dollar bill. Invite children to use the giant money to share their understanding of money relationships with the class.

◆ Make up problems for children to solve with the giant magnetic money. You might present problems that involve a family of giants and their earning and spending activities. If desired, have children write the problems on paper (or the mini math boards from page 44) in order to practice writing in monetary units.

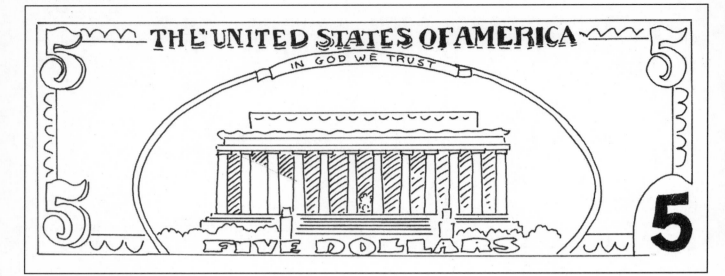

Magnetic Coin Keepers

Reinforce money concepts with these magnetic coin trays.

Materials

- coin patterns, page 88
- crayons
- round or square iron or steel stove-burner cover per child (light, solid colors work best)
- laminator
- scissors
- magnetic tape
- black fine-point permanent marker

Skills and Concepts

- coin recognition
- money values
- problem-solving

Making the Magnetic Coin Keepers

1 Decide which coins—and the quantity of each—that you want to include in one coin set. (Make sure all the coins will fit on one half of the stove-burner cover without overlapping.) Then copy the money patterns as many times as needed to create a coin set for each stove-burner cover to be used.

2 Color the coins to resemble real money. Laminate and cut out the coins.

3 Back each coin with magnetic tape.

4 To make a coin keeper, turn each stove-burner cover over so that it resembles a tray. Use the permanent marker to draw a straight line across the middle of the coin keeper. Then place a set of coins in the coin keeper, spacing them evenly across one side of the coin keeper.

5 When you have the coins positioned as desired, use the permanent marker to trace the outline of each one onto the coin keeper.

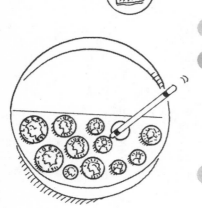

HANDY HINTS

▲ If a laminator is not available, cover the coins with clear plastic adhesive covering.

▲ If desired, use the individual magnetic coin keepers with the giant magnetic coins on page 85.

▲ You may wish to use real or plastic play-money coins in the coin keepers. Simply attach a piece of magnetic tape to each plastic coin to be used.

▲ For a larger workspace, children can turn their coin keepers over and attach their coins to the unmarked side.

Ways to Use the Magnetic Coin Keepers

◆ Have children remove all the coins from their coin keepers. Then call out a coin name, such as penny or nickel. Ask students to find the named coin and place it on a corresponding outline. Then have them tell the value of the coin. Encourage children to find both front and back versions of the specified coin.

◆ Ask children to place designated groups of silver coins into their coin keepers, such as nickels or dimes. Then have them skip-count to find the value of all the coins.

◆ Call out a money amount that can be produced with the set of coins in the coin keeper. Challenge children to arrange a combination of coins equal to the given amount in the open half of their coin keepers. Have them hold up their coin keepers to show you their work (the magnetic tape should hold the coins in place). Later, invite student partners to take turns calling out money amounts and arranging coins in their coin keepers to equal the named amount.

◆ Use the coins and coin keeper to help children understand the relationship between the different coins. For example, you might ask them to put five nickels in their coin keepers and then add another single coin that is equal to the value of the nickels (one quarter).

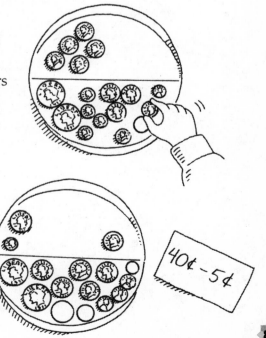

◆ Make up problems for children to solve with their coin keepers. You can present simple addition, subtraction, multiplication, and division problems, as well as word problems and problems involving money conversion. Make sure the problems can be solved with the coin set in students' coin keepers. You may also wish to have children write the problems and answers on paper to give them practice writing in monetary units.

Jiffy Geometric Wallpaper Squares

These quick and easy-to-make wallpaper squares can be used to reinforce geometry concepts and much more!

Materials

- wallpaper sample books
- scissors

Making the Jiffy Geometric Wallpaper Squares

1. Flip through the wallpaper book to find samples with repeating patterns. Carefully remove these samples from the book.

2. Group the samples by the size of their repeating patterns. For instance, the samples with large repeating patterns will be grouped together, and those with small patterns will be grouped.

3. Cut each group of wallpaper samples into squares that contain several repetitions of the pattern.

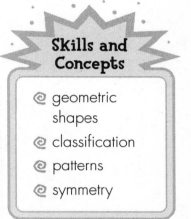

Skills and Concepts

- geometric shapes
- classification
- patterns
- symmetry

HANDY HINTS

▲ Check with home decorating stores to ask for donations or reduced prices for outdated wallpaper sample books. You may also request that parents and other staff members donate leftover wallpaper to your class.

▲ In addition to wallpaper, you can also use wallpaper border for this project.

Ways to Use the Jiffy Geometric Wallpaper Squares

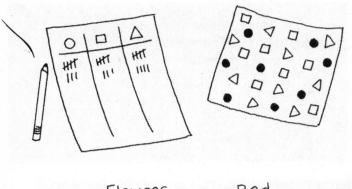

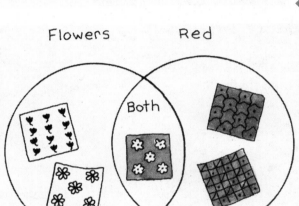

Flowers   Red

Both

◆ Challenge children to find as many geometric shapes as possible in a selection of wallpaper squares. Have them count the number of different shapes found and report their results. Or have children graph the different geometric shapes found on a single wallpaper square.

◆ Reinforce classification skills with the wallpaper squares. To do this, present children with one or more attributes to look for in the squares. Then have them sort the squares according to whether or not the attributes apply to the patterns. Alternatively, you can set up a simple Venn diagram for children to complete using the wallpaper squares. For example, your Venn diagram might be labeled "Flowers" for one circle, "Red" for the other, and "Both" for the overlapping section.

◆ For patterning practice, have children match wallpaper squares with identical patterns. Or give children wallpaper squares, paper, and crayons. Then have them draw a continuation of the wallpaper pattern on the paper. To extend, you can invite children to create their own repeating patterns on paper squares.

◆ Give children a supply of wallpaper squares containing sets with identical patterns. Invite children to create a "quilt" with a repeating pattern of wallpaper squares.

◆ Provide students with square hand mirrors. Then invite them to use the mirrors with the wallpaper squares to look for symmetrical and asymmetrical designs as well as patterns.

◆ Have children measure the length or width of the repeating pattern on a wallpaper square. Then have them calculate how many repetitions of that pattern will fit on a surface of a given size, such as a book or tabletop.

Terrific Tiles

Cover a range of geometry and other math skills with these versatile floor designs.

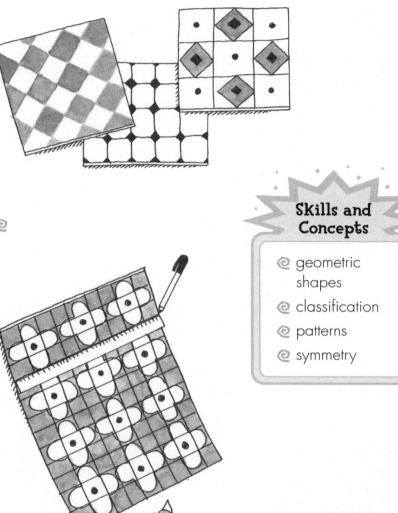

Materials

- linoleum tile squares (and samples of linoleum sheets) in various colors and patterns
- yardstick
- pen
- heavy-duty scissors

Making the Terrific Tiles

1 If you plan to use both linoleum tile squares and linoleum sheets, use the yardstick and pen to measure and mark the sheets to the size of the tiles (usually 12 inches square). As you mark the sheeting, make sure you include the full pattern in each section. To accomplish this for some floor patterns, you might have to measure larger pieces.

2 Use the heavy-duty scissors to cut out each linoleum square from the sheeting.

Skills and Concepts

- geometric shapes
- classification
- patterns
- symmetry

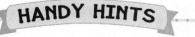

──── **HANDY HINTS** ────

▲ Often, flooring stores are willing to donate discontinued linoleum samples and remnants or sell them at a discount.

Ways to Use the Terrific Tiles

◆ Challenge children to find as many different geometric shapes as possible in the tiles. Ask them to count the number of each shape on one tile and report their findings. Or have children graph the different geometric shapes found on a single tile.

◆ Reinforce classification skills with the tiles. Have children examine the tiles for a given characteristic, such as a color, shape, or symmetrical design. Ask them to sort the tiles according to whether or not they share the characteristic. Alternatively, you can set up a simple Venn diagram for children to complete using the tiles. For example, your Venn diagram might be labeled "White Squares" for one circle, "Blue Flowers" for the other, and "Both" for the overlapping section.

◆ For patterning practice, have children match tiles with identical patterns. Or ask them to draw a continuation of a particular tile pattern on paper. To extend, invite children to create their own repeating tile patterns on paper squares.

◆ Ask children to sort the tiles with symmetrical patterns from the rest of the tiles. Then have them explain how the pattern shows symmetry. Invite them to create their own paper tiles with symmetrical patterns.

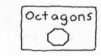

Octagons

◆ Have students use the tiles to create a bar graph. First, ask them to make column labels such as "Squares," "Triangles," and "Octagons" by writing each heading on a sheet of paper. Have students place the labels on the floor and then graph a group of tiles. When students have finished, ask them to tally and report their results.

Necktie Pattern Busy Board

Accessorize students' math skills with this assortment of patterned neckties.

Materials

- clean neckties with various patterns (geometric shapes, stripes, checks, and so on)
- large dry-erase board
- clothespins (or binder clips)
- wipe-off pens
- paper towels

Making the Necktie Pattern Busy Board

1 Select one or more neckties to use to reinforce the desired skill (finding repeating patterns or symmetrical designs, matching shapes, and so on).

2 Drape each selected necktie over the dry-erase board so that the wide part of the tie is on the front of the board. Use a clothespin (or binder clip) to secure the tie to the top of the board.

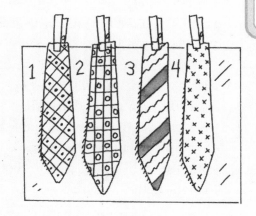

3 If desired, use a wipe-off pen to write a number reference beside each tie attached to the board.

Skills and Concepts

- patterns
- symmetry
- classification

HANDY HINTS

▲ If desired, secure the bottom of each tie to the board with clear, wide tape.

▲ You may wish to hang and store the unused ties on coat hangers, securing them with clothespins.

▲ Collect neckties from parents, staff members, and even your own closet. Most men are very willing to part with their older neckties for a good cause!

Ways to Use the Necktie Pattern Busy Board

◆ Challenge children to find as many geometric shapes as possible in the ties on the board. Have them count the number of different shapes found and report their results. To extend, children can use the wipe-off pens to draw each geometric shape found on a tie on the board beside the tie.

◆ Name a characteristic of one or more of the ties on the board. Have children find the tie(s) with the named attribute. For example, you might ask students to find all the ties with stripes, a red repeating triangle pattern, or a symmetrical design. To reinforce specific skills, such as finding patterns with similar attributes, be sure to display ties with appropriate designs. If you labeled the ties on the board, encourage children to refer to each one by its number.

◆ Place a single tie with a repeating pattern or symmetrical design on the board. Invite children to use colored wipe-off pens to duplicate the design on the board.

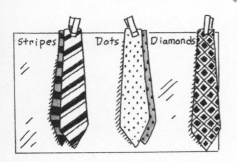

◆ Reinforce classification skills with the necktie board. To do this, remove all the ties and write several different attributes across the top of the board. Have children sort ties by the given attributes. When finished, have them attach the ties to the board next to their respective labels. Then ask children to explain the reasoning behind their classification method. Alternatively, you can draw a simple Venn diagram on the board and label it with attributes of the ties. For example, you might label one circle "Trees," the other circle "Green," and the overlapping section "Both." Have children use the ties to complete the diagram.

◆ Place the board on a flat surface. Using a wipe-off pen, draw a simple graph on the board and label each column with a shape, color, design description, or other characteristic of the ties to be used. Then give students a supply of ties to graph on the board. When finished, have children tally and report the results to the class.

◆ Invite children to use the ties as informal units of measure to measure large objects and areas, such as bookshelves and the length of the classroom. Ask them to write their findings on the board and display the number of ties used in their measurements. Have children compare their work.

Geometric Holiday Ornaments

Deck the halls—and students' math learning—with these jolly geometric ornaments.

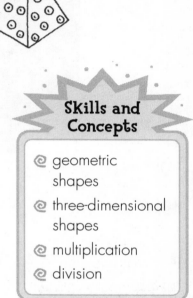

Materials

- ■ cube and pyramid patterns, pages 97–98
- ■ 9- by 12-inch piece of colored posterboard for each ornament to be made
- ■ pencil with dull point
- ■ scissors
- ■ glue
- ■ string or yarn
- ■ glitter pens
- ■ sequins
- ■ glitter

Skills and Concepts

- ☺ geometric shapes
- ☺ three-dimensional shapes
- ☺ multiplication
- ☺ division

Making the Geometric Holiday Ornaments

1 Trace the pattern of your choice onto a piece of posterboard. Trace both the outline and the dotted lines, applying enough pressure with the pencil to leave impressions of the dotted lines on the posterboard. Cut out the shape.

2 Fold along the line impressions on the posterboard cutout and glue down all the flaps to form the three-dimensional shape (either a cube or pyramid). If desired, use the fold lines on the pattern as a reference for folding the shape.

3 To make a hanger, trap a string or yarn loop in a corner of the shape while the glue is still wet.

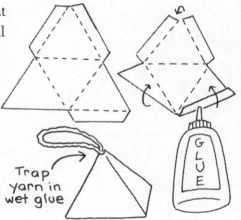

Trap yarn in wet glue

4 After the shape has dried thoroughly, decorate it as desired with glitter pens, sequins, or glitter.

5 Make several models of each shape to use with the activities provided. When not in use, add the shapes to a holiday display.

HANDY HINTS

▲ In addition to posterboard, you might make the shapes from other materials such as wallpaper, sheets of corrugated paper, or thick pieces of decorative wrapping paper.

▲ If desired, enlarge the patterns to make different-size shapes.

▲ Invite children to create and decorate geometric holiday ornaments to display around the classroom or give as gifts.

Ways to Use the Geometric Holiday Ornaments

◆ Ask children to examine and discuss their observations of each holiday ornament shape. Have them name the shape of the sides and then count the number of sides and corners on each ornament. Invite children to tell ways in which the two ornaments are similar and different.

◆ Show children the patterns for the pyramid and cube. Explain that the patterns have two dimensions—length and width—so they are called two-dimensional. Then demonstrate how to fold the pattern to create the pyramid and cube. Tell children that these shapes are three-dimensional because they have length, width, and depth. Point out each dimension. Afterward, give children a pattern for each shape and have them construct the three-dimensional shapes. Encourage them to identify each dimension on their completed shapes.

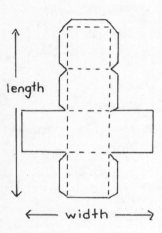

length

width

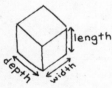

length
depth
width

◆ Create a three-column chart, labeling the first column "Number of Shapes," the second "Number of Sides per Shape," and the last "Total Number of Sides." Then give children a collection of each ornament shape. Have them use the shapes to fill in the chart. Use the information to show children a multiplication "shortcut" to finding the total number of sides. Presenting sets of different quantities of ornament shapes, have children continue filling in the chart. Each time, help them perform the multiplication for finding the total number of sides. If desired, have them write and solve each problem on paper as well. (You may also wish to reorder the columns and then use the chart to reinforce division skills.)

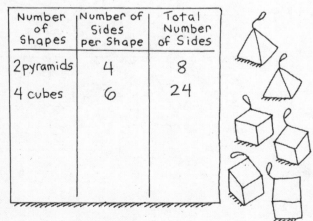

Number of Shapes	Number of Sides per Shape	Total Number of Sides
2 pyramids	4	8
4 cubes	6	24

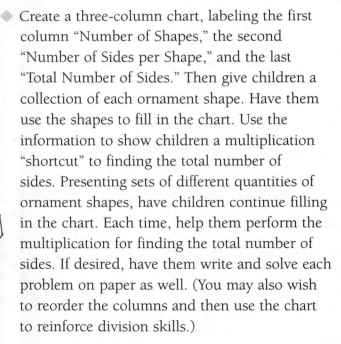

Cube Pattern

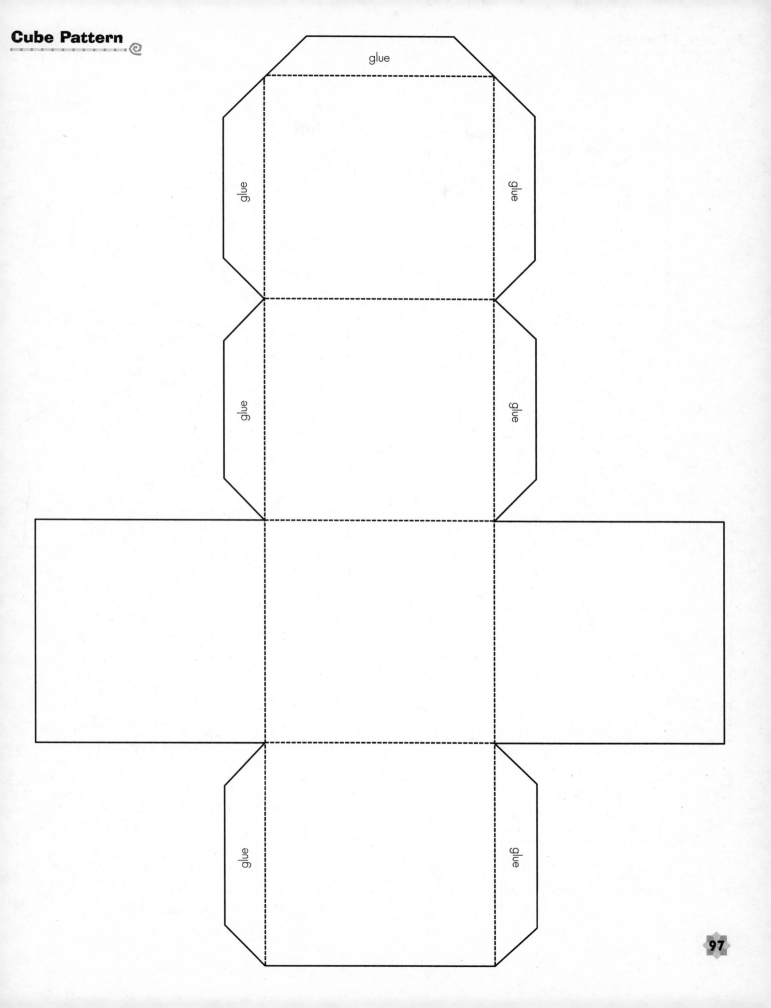

glue

glue

glue

glue

glue

glue

glue

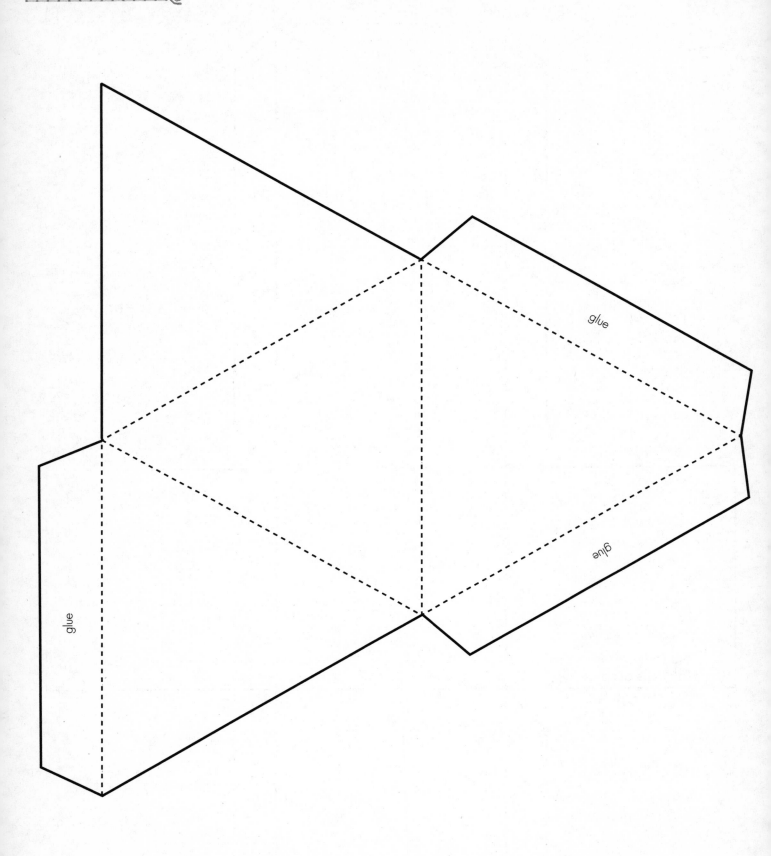

glue

glue

glue

Individual Geoboards

These low-cost geoboards provide valuable hands-on experience with shapes, patterns, and other math concepts.

Materials

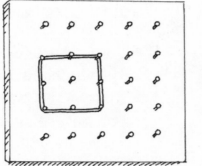

- 6-inch square of $\frac{1}{2}$-inch plywood (one per student)
- fine-grade sandpaper
- ruler
- pencil
- 25 1-inch finishing nails for each board
- hammer
- assortment of rubber bands

Making the Individual Geoboards

1 Sand each plywood square to smooth the surface and edges.

2 Use a pencil and ruler to draw a one-inch grid on each plywood square. When finished, you will have 25 intersecting lines on the board.

3 Hammer a nail into the board at each point where two lines intersect. Make sure you drive the nails deep into the wood.

Skills and Concepts

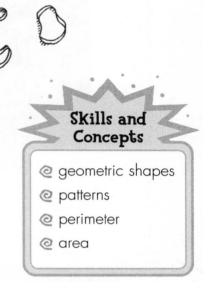

- geometric shapes
- patterns
- perimeter
- area

HANDY HINTS

▲ If desired, spray-paint the boards with the paint color of your choice or a clear acrylic varnish. Be sure to paint the boards outdoors or in a well-ventilated area. Allow the paint to dry thoroughly before use.

▲ In addition to the six-inch square, you may wish to make one or more larger geoboards (for example, a 12-inch square) for student use.

Ways to Use the Individual Geoboards

◆ Have children use rubber bands to create a variety of geometric shapes on their geoboards. After forming each shape, ask them to name and then reproduce the shape on paper or another geoboard.

◆ Working in pairs, have one student create a rubber band shape or pattern on a geoboard. Then ask his or her partner to reproduce the shape or pattern on another board. Have children take turns creating and reproducing geoboard designs.

◆ To reinforce the difference between squares and rectangles, call out the name of one of the shapes. Then ask children to create the named shape on their geoboards. Afterward, help them measure the length and width of their shapes by counting the spaces between the nails along each side. Have them use their findings to determine whether or not they created the correct shape.

◆ Have children create squares and rectangles on their geoboards. Then ask them to count the spaces between the nails for each side of their shapes. Have children use their results to find the perimeter and area of their shapes. If desired, ask children to write and solve their problems on paper and then have a classmate check their work.

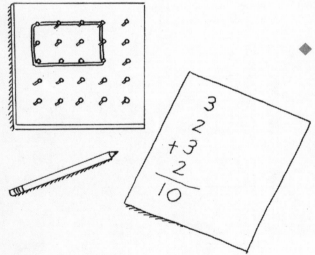

Giant Fraction Magnets

Use these large fraction magnets to teach children about part-to-whole concepts and relationships.

Materials

- 3 copies each of the fraction circle 1 and 2 patterns, pages 103–104
- 7 colored plastic plates
- tape
- black fine-point permanent marker
- ruler
- scissors
- black wide-tip permanent marker
- magnetic tape
- magnetic chalkboard or display board

Skills and Concepts

- simple fractions
- fraction names
- equivalent fractions
- operations with fractions

Making the Giant Fraction Magnets

1. To divide the plates into fractions, tape a fraction circle pattern to the center of all but one plate (this plate will represent a whole, or 1). Sort the plates into two piles, circle 1 and circle 2.

2. On the first circle 1 plate, extend the solid line (marked $\frac{1}{2}$ on the pattern) to the plate rim using the ruler and fine-point marker. Cut the plate along the extended line, cutting through the pattern and plate.

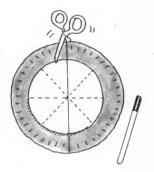

3. For the second circle 1 plate, extend the lines for $\frac{1}{2}$ and $\frac{1}{4}$ to the plate rim. Then cut along these lines to create quarter sections of the plate. Repeat for the last circle 1 plate, drawing extended lines on the plate for all of the lines on the pattern. Cut this plate into the eight marked sections.

4. Repeat steps 2 and 3 for the circle 2 plates, drawing and cutting along the marked lines to create plates divided into thirds, sixths, and twelfths.

5. Remove the pattern from each plate section and use the wide-tip marker to label it with the corresponding fraction, such as $\frac{1}{2}$, $\frac{1}{4}$, $\frac{1}{8}$, $\frac{1}{3}$, $\frac{1}{6}$, or $\frac{1}{12}$. Label the uncut plate "1."

6. Back each plate section with magnetic tape. Make sure the magnet will support the weight of the section when it is placed on the magnetic board.

HANDY HINTS

▲ If desired, make several magnetic fraction sets to use for teaching mixed fractions with numbers larger than one.

▲ You may wish to use paper plates in different colors if you cannot find plastic plates.

Ways to Use the Giant Fraction Magnets

◆ Use chalk to trace the whole plate on the board. Explain to students that a whole can be made of many equal parts. Then give them one set of fractions at a time to fit into the circle outline. Tell children the name of each fraction section as they fit it into the circle (for instance, one-half, one-third, or one-sixth). To extend, show children how to write addition equations with the fractions. Use this opportunity to explain that when the numerator and denominator are the same number (such as $\frac{12}{12}$), the fraction equals a whole, or 1.

◆ Using the circle outline and fraction sets, have children fit different fraction combinations into the circle to complete the whole. For example, they can fill the circle with one $\frac{1}{2}$, one $\frac{1}{4}$, and two $\frac{1}{8}$ sections. As children work with this activity, guide them to discover how the different-size fraction sections relate to each other as well as to the whole circle. Ask them to write equations to show these relationships (for instance, $\frac{1}{4} + \frac{1}{4} = \frac{1}{2}$).

◆ Use the fraction sets to present subtraction problems for children to solve. To do this, place all of the sections of one set, such as the thirds, in a chalk circle. Then take away one section and have children name the fraction for the remaining sections. To reinforce writing equations with fractions, have children write these problems and solutions on paper.

◆ Demonstrate how to multiply fractions by using a repeated addition format. First, present a multiplication problem, such as 5 x $\frac{1}{6}$. Then show children how to add five of the $\frac{1}{6}$ sections together to arrive at the answer. After children understand the method, present similar practice problems for children to solve on their own with the fraction magnets. Conversely, children can solve division problems with fractions by using a repeated subtraction format.

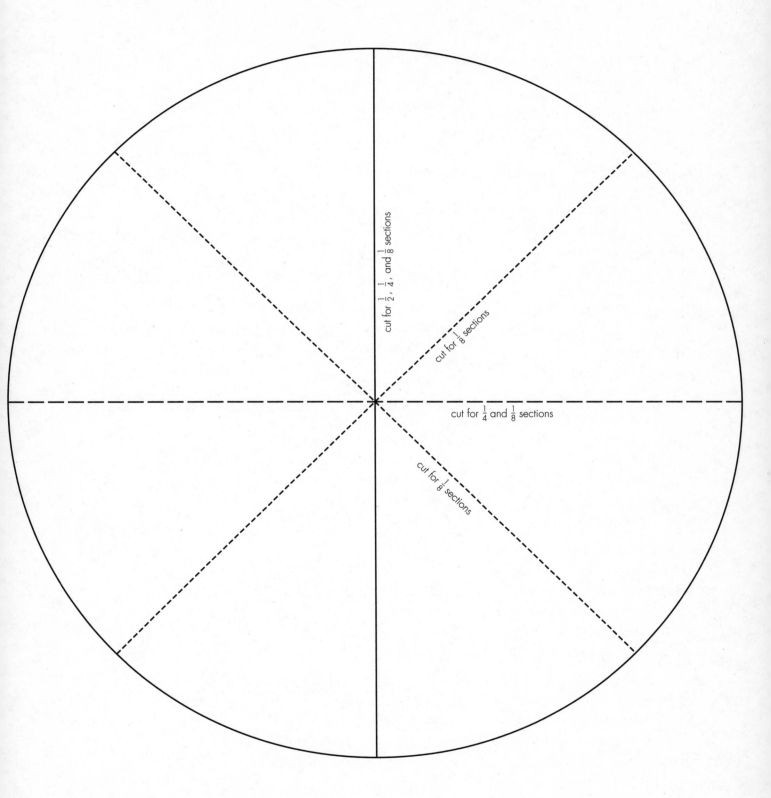

cut for $\frac{1}{2}$, $\frac{1}{4}$, and $\frac{1}{8}$ sections

cut for $\frac{1}{8}$ sections

cut for $\frac{1}{4}$ and $\frac{1}{8}$ sections

cut for $\frac{1}{8}$ sections

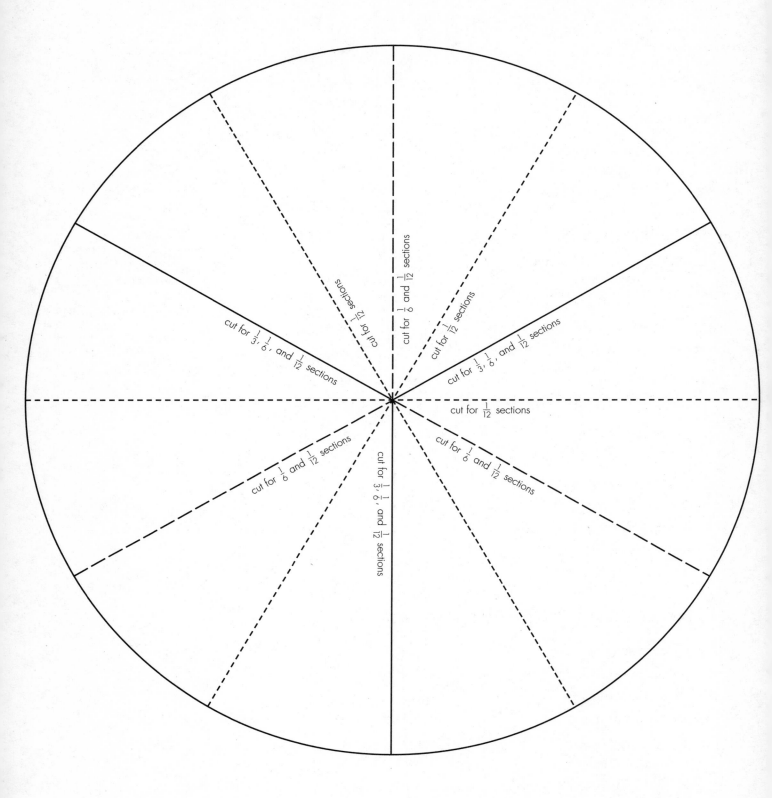

cut for $\frac{1}{6}$ and $\frac{1}{12}$ sections

cut for $\frac{1}{12}$ sections

cut for $\frac{1}{3}$, $\frac{1}{6}$, and $\frac{1}{12}$ sections

cut for $\frac{1}{12}$ sections

cut for $\frac{1}{3}$, $\frac{1}{6}$, and $\frac{1}{12}$ sections

cut for $\frac{1}{12}$ sections

cut for $\frac{1}{6}$ and $\frac{1}{12}$ sections

cut for $\frac{1}{6}$ and $\frac{1}{12}$ sections

cut for $\frac{1}{3}$, $\frac{1}{6}$, and $\frac{1}{12}$ sections

Linoleum Dominoes

A long line of math concept and reasoning skills can be taught with these unique blocks.

Materials

- 1- by 3½-foot strip of linoleum in a light, solid color (this will be enough to make 28 domino tiles)
- ruler
- heavy-duty scissors
- black fine-point permanent marker

Making the Linoleum Dominoes

1. Use the ruler and marker to divide the linoleum strip into 3- by 6-inch rectangles.

2. Cut the rectangles apart with heavy-duty scissors. When finished, you will have 28 domino tiles.

3. Use the permanent marker to draw a line across the middle of each tile.

4. Decide on a concept to reinforce with the dominoes. Then label the tiles with items related to the selected concept. Use the diagram as a guide to labeling the dominoes to make sure each end has a corresponding match.

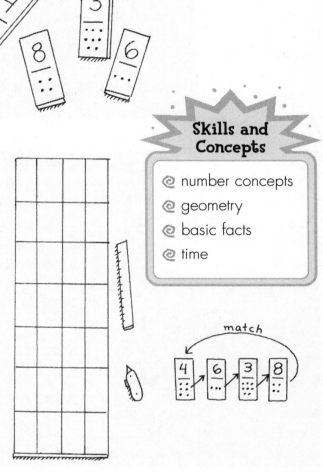

Skills and Concepts

- number concepts
- geometry
- basic facts
- time

HANDY HINTS

⊳ Use these suggestions to label the linoleum dominoes:

- Label one end with a shape name and the other with a drawing of a different shape.
- Write a numeral on one end and a different number name on the other.
- Label one end of a domino with a basic addition or subtraction fact. Write the answer to a different fact on the opposite end of the tile.
- Stamp a clock face on 2½-inch paper squares. Fill in a different time on each clock and then attach each one to a domino. Label the opposite end of each tile with a time that corresponds to one of the other clocks.

▲ If possible, use linoleum that is pre-marked with 3-inch squares. This will eliminate the need to measure and mark the piece for cutting. Or you may wish to use four 12-inch linoleum squares (without the adhesive backing).

▲ If desired, make additional domino tiles for your set. Or make several sets from different linoleum colors. You may wish to make a blank set that allows for flexible labeling. Simply label this set with a wipe-off pen, then "erase" the tiles with a paper towel when you're ready to program them with a different skill.

Ways to Use the Linoleum Dominoes

◆ To play dominoes, distribute the tiles evenly to a small group of children. Then decide the order in which players will take turns. The first player places a tile faceup on the table. The second player tries to match one end of the displayed domino with a tile from his or her hand. If the child does not have a match, play progresses to the next player. Players take turns matching the dominoes end to end until no more matches can be made. The first player to use all of his or her dominoes wins the round.

◆ Distribute the dominoes to children. Have them trace the tiles on paper and cut out the shapes. Then ask them to label their paper dominoes with skills that correspond to their linoleum dominoes. For example, for a number-recognition domino with one end labeled "three" and the other "8," a child will create a paper domino labeled "3" at one end and "eight" on the other end.

◆ Invite children to use the dominoes to create their own matching games. For example, they might distribute the tiles among themselves. Then players work together to find the matches to all the tiles.

Probability Clothes Dryer

Chances are students will learn a lot about probability with this cardboard box clothes dryer.

Materials

- medium-size cardboard box (approximately 1-foot square)
- glue
- craft knife
- pencil
- ruler
- 3-inch-wide cardboard strip the length of the box sides
- wide, clear tape
- plastic adhesive covering in a solid color
- black permanent marker
- 6 socks (3 of one color, 2 of a second color, and 1 of a third color)

Skills and Concepts

- chance
- probability
- predictions

Making the Probability Clothes Dryer

1 Close and glue the top flaps of the box in place.

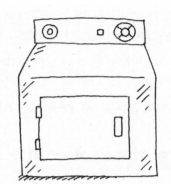

2 After the glue has dried, turn the box over and use the bottom for the top of the dryer. Use the ruler and pencil to draw a door on one side of the box. Then cut out three sides of the door with a craft knife, creating a "hinged" door that can be opened and closed.

3 Use the wide tape to attach the cardboard strip to the top back of the dryer. This piece will serve as a control panel for the dryer.

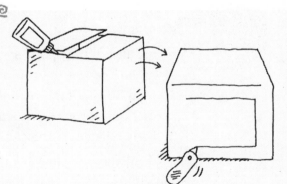

4 Cover the entire surface of the dryer with the plastic adhesive covering. Using the craft knife, carefully cut through the covering along the three sides of the door.

5 If desired, cover the inside of the dryer door with plastic covering.

6 Use the permanent marker to draw dials on the control panel and a handle and hinges on the door.

107

HANDY HINTS

▲ If bubbles appear in the plastic adhesive covering, "pop" them by poking them with the end of a straight pin and using your fingers to press the air out.

▲ To create a dryer with a window, cut a hole in the middle of the door. After you cover the dryer with plastic adhesive covering, cut out the hole again. Then tape a clear transparency over the hole on the inside of the door to create a window.

▲ If desired, use a hot glue gun to attach plastic milk-jug lids and a soda-bottle lid to create the dryer knobs and door handle.

▲ To add variety, use an assortment of clothing for the suggested activities.

Ways to Use the Probability Clothes Dryer

◆ Place only the three same-color socks in the dryer. Ask children to predict what sock color you will pull out. Have them explain their reasoning. Then tumble the socks in the dryer, and remove one sock. Did children predict the correct color? Repeat the procedure a few more times. Afterward, explain that because the three socks are the same color, there is a 3 out of 3 chance (a certain chance) that you will draw out a sock of that color.

◆ Replace one of the socks in the activity above with a different color sock. Ask children to predict whether it is more likely or unlikely that you'll pull out a sock of the first color. Ask them to explain their responses. Then tumble the socks, and remove one sock. Make a note of the color, return the sock to the dryer, and repeat the procedure until it has been done five times, and then 10, 20, and 30 times. Have children review the results at each interval. Were their predictions correct? Explain that, in this example, there is a 2 out of 3 chance (a likely chance) that a sock of the first color will be selected.

◆ Place all six socks in the clothes dryer. Ask children to predict what color sock you will pull out. After they share their reasoning, tumble the socks in the dryer, open the door, and remove one sock. Make a note of the color, return the sock, and repeat the procedure four more times. At this point, ask children to predict what color sock you will pull out next. Repeat the procedure 10, 20, and then 30 times, and keep a tally of the results. Encourage children to revise their predictions as the process continues. Afterward, help them analyze the results. Which predictions were most accurate—those made after just a few, or after many trials? Guide children to understand that, only by doing many trials, do they collect enough data to make more accurate predictions. If desired, help children determine the actual probability of pulling out each sock color (3 out of 6 for the first color, 2 out of 6 for the second, and 1 out of 6 for the third).

Velcro Bar Graph

Graphing skills are sure to stick with students with this unique bar graph.

Materials

■ 2 posterboards, one in a light color and the other in a contrasting color
■ yardstick
■ pencil
■ laminator
■ scissors
■ several self-adhesive rolls of Velcro
■ wipe-off marker

Skills and Concepts

◉ graphing
◉ categorization
◉ skip-counting

Making the Velcro Bar Graph

1 Use the yardstick and pencil to mark the contrasting posterboard into 2-inch squares. Laminate both posterboards.

2 Cut four lengths of Velcro hook equal to the length of the light-colored posterboard. Attach the four strips to the posterboard, starting two inches from each side and spacing them evenly across the posterboard.

3 Cut the contrasting poster into squares, as marked. You (or students) will label these "graph" squares with words or pictures related to the topic to be graphed.

4 Attach a piece of Velcro loop to one side of each 2-inch posterboard square.

5 To use the Velcro bar graph, turn it either horizontally or vertically. Use the wipe-off marker to write a heading for each column (or row, depending on the graph's orientation) on a graph square. Or attach a picture to represent the heading. Attach the headings to the graph; then have children place their labeled graph squares with the appropriate headings on the graph.

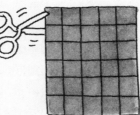

HANDY HINTS

▲ If a laminator is not available, cover the posterboard in clear plastic adhesive covering.

▲ Cutting the posterboard into small squares can be simplified by using a large paper cutter if one is available.

▲ You may wish to make graphing pieces from felt or flannel since both of these materials also stick to Velcro.

Ways to Use the Velcro Bar Graph

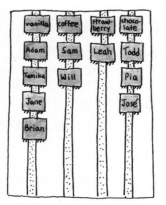

◆ To graph student preferences, label the graph columns with color names, ice cream flavors, sports, or similar categories of your choice. Then have children write their names on the graph squares and attach them to the column (or row) labeled with their preferences. When the graph is completed, have children tally and discuss the results.

◆ Label the graph columns with different weather conditions. Then invite children to attach graph squares to graph the weather for a given period of time. Have them tally the results to determine which weather conditions were most prominent during the graphing period.

◆ Have children practice categorizing skills with the Velcro graph. First, label the columns with the desired headings, such as "Bird," "Mammal," "Fish," and "Reptile." Then give children a supply of the graph squares labeled with the items to be graphed, in this instance, the names or pictures of different animals from each category. After children graph their squares, have them review and discuss the results.

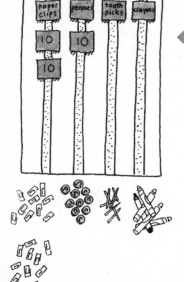

◆ To practice skip-counting and help children understand how to use a scale in graphing activities, give them several sets of objects in multiples of ten, such as paper clips, toothpicks, and pennies. Label the graph columns with the name of each object. Then explain that when graphing large numbers of objects, a scale is often used. Ask children to divide each set into groups of 10, and then assign a graph square to each group (they can use the wipe-off marker to make 10 marks on each square, if desired). After students graph the squares, have them tally their results by counting the squares by tens. For additional practice, have children graph items using scales of different sizes, such as threes, fives, or hundreds.